Ballads of Robin Hood and other Outlaws; Popular Ballads of the Olden Times - Fourth Series

Frank Sidgwick

Alpha Editions

This edition published in 2024

ISBN : 9789366387345

Design and Setting By
Alpha Editions
www.alphaedis.com
Email - info@alphaedis.com

As per information held with us this book is in Public Domain.
This book is a reproduction of an important historical work. Alpha Editions uses the best technology to reproduce historical work in the same manner it was first published to preserve its original nature. Any marks or number seen are left intentionally to preserve its true form.

PREFACE

THIS volume concludes the series, begun in 1903, which was intended to comprise all the best traditional ballads of England and Scotland. The scheme of classification by subject-matter, arbitrary and haphazard as it may seem to be at one point or another, has, I think, proved more satisfactory than could have been anticipated; and in the end I have omitted no ballad without due justification.

In the fourteen years which have elapsed since the completion of Professor Child's collection, there has been discovered, so far as I know, only one ballad that can claim the right to be added to his roll of 305 'English and Scottish Popular Ballads.' That one is the carol of *The Bitter Withy*, which I was fortunate enough to recover in 1905, which my friend Professor Gerould of Princeton University has annotated with an erudition worthy of Child, and the genuineness of which has been sponsored by viii Professor Gummere.1 I should perhaps have included this in its place in my Second Series, had I known of it in time, but I still hope to treat the traditional English Carols separately. I ought to admit here that the confidence with which I claimed, in my Third Series, a place on the roll for *The Jolly Juggler*, has abated, and I now consider it to be no more than a narrative lyric without any definitely 'popular' characteristics.

These four volumes contain in all 143 ballads, four of which are not to be found in Child's collection.2 Thus, out of his 305, I have omitted more than half; but it must be remembered that his work was a collection, and mine—*si parva licet componere magnis*—has been selection. The omitted ballads are either:—

(i) Fragmentary or mutilated;

(ii) Closely related to ballads which I include;

(iii) Uninteresting, *e.g.* as dealing with obscure history;

(iv) Degenerate.

The last reason for exclusion particularly affects the Robin Hood ballads, among which ix Child prints thirty-three late broadsides and fragments which I omit. He preferred to err by inclusion rather than exclusion, and states that he has admitted more than one ballad, 'actually worthless and manifestly spurious, because of a remote possibility that it might contain relics, or be a debased representative, of something genuine and better.'3

I cannot take leave of nine years' intermittent work on this selection without remembering that its 'only begetter' was Mr. A. H. Bullen, with whom I published the first three volumes. While I regret to think how different it is in the result from the edition he then envisaged, I gratefully acknowledge my indebtedness to him for the inoculation. The anthologist is strictly a plucker of the flowers of literature; but the ballads are not literature—they are lore, and therefore of warmer human interest.

F. S.

[1] *The Popular Ballad* (1907), p. 228.

[2] These are *The Nutbrown Maid*, First Series; The *Lyke-Wake Dirge* and *Adam*, Second Series; and *The Jolly Juggler*, Third Series.

[3] Vol. v. p. 182.

INTRODUCTION TO THE ROBIN HOOD BALLADS

'It is our olde manner,' sayd Robyn,

'To leve but lytell behynde.'

'IT will scarcely be expected that one should be able to offer an authentic narrative of the life and transactions of this extraordinary personage. The times in which he lived, the mode of life he adopted, and the silence or loss of contemporary writers, are circumstances sufficiently favourable, indeed, to romance, but altogether inimical to historical truth.' In these words Joseph Ritson, the first and most painstaking of those well-meaning scholars who have tried to associate the outlaw with 'historical truth,' begins his 'Life of Robin Hood,' an account which occupies ten pages of his book, and is annotated and illustrated through the following one hundred and five pages. The *Dictionary of National Biography* includes Robin Hood, as it includes King Arthur; but it is better to face the truth, and to state boldly that Robin Hood the yeoman outlaw never existed in the flesh. As the goddess Athena sprang from the head of Zeus, Robin Hood sprang from the imagination of the English people.

That being so, he is a creation of whom the English people, who have kept him so long alive where he was born and bred, should be proud; and after reflecting on his essential characteristics—his love of the poor, his courteous robbery of the higher orders both spiritual and temporal, his loyalty to the king, his freedom with the king's deer, and his esteem of all women for the sake of the Virgin—an Englishman should be the first to resent any attempt to identify so truly popular a hero either with one of several historical nonentities, or with a member of the aristocracy, or worst of all, with an Aryan sun-myth.

All these attempts have been made at one time or another, but not until the spirit which begot him had begun to dwindle in the English heart. If King Arthur is the ideal knight of Celtic chivalry, Robin is the ideal champion of the popular cause under feudal conditions: his enemies are bishops, fat monks, and the sheriff who would restrain his liberty. It is natural that an enfranchised yeoman, who took toll of the oppressors, and so effected what we still call xiii a redistribution of wealth, should be the hero of the oppressed and the law-abiding poor; and it is natural that, as social conditions altered (for better or for worse) with the national prosperity under Elizabeth, and classes and masses reconsidered their relative positions, Robin should fall from the popular pantheon, and should degenerate, as we find him degenerated in the broadsides of the Reformation hacks, into a swashbuckler unheroic enough to be defeated in quarter-staff bouts and so undemocratic as to find for himself a noble title and a wife of high degree.

There are, then, four Robin Hoods:—

(i) The popular outlaw of the greenwood, as revealed to us in the older ballads.

(ii) The quasi-historical Robin, the outlaw ennobled (by a contradiction in terms) as the Earl of Huntingdon, Robert Fitzooth, etc., and the husband of Matilda.

(iii) One of a number of actual Robert Hoods, whose existence (and insignificance) has been proved from historical documents.

(iv) Robin Hood, or Robin o' Wood, explained by German scholars as the English representative of Woden, or a wood-god, or some other mythical personage.

We will now investigate these in turn, attempting so far as may be possible to keep them distinct.

I. THE BALLAD HERO ROBIN HOOD

The earliest known reference to Robin Hood the outlaw was first pointed out by Bishop Percy, the editor of the *Reliques*, in *Piers Plowman*, the poem written by Langland about 1377, where Sloth says (B. text, passus v. 401):—

'But I can [know] rymes of Robyn hood, and Randolf erle of Chestre.'

Observing that this first mention of Robin is as the subject of ballads, and that he is coupled with another popular hero, one of the twelfth-century Earls of Chester, we pass to the next reference.

> 'Lytill Ihon and Robyne Hude
>
> Waythmen ware commendyd gude;
>
> In Yngilwode and Barnysdale
>
> Thai oysyd all this tyme thare trawale.'

This passage, from Wyntoun's *Chronicle of Scotland* (about 1420), is referred to the year 1283, and means that Robin and his man Little John were known as good hunters (cf. 'wight yeomen,' constantly in the ballads), and they carried on their business in Inglewood and Barnsdale at this time.

In 1439 a petition was presented to Parliament concerning a certain Piers Venables, of whom it is stated that, having no other livelihood, he 'gadered and assembled unto him many misdoers' and 'wente into the wodes in that contrë, like as it hadde be Robyn-hode and his meynë.'

About the same time (c. 1437), a longer description is given in Fordun's *Scotichronicon*, which was revised and continued by Bower, where the latter states that Robin Hood, 'that most celebrated robber,' was one of the dispossessed and banished followers of Simon de Montfort. He proceeds, however, to couple with him 'Litill Johanne' and their associates, 'of whom the foolish vulgar in comedies and tragedies make lewd entertainment, and are delighted to hear the jesters and minstrels sing them above all other ballads,'4 and to describe briefly one of the 'tragedies.'

An extract from one more chronicler will suffice, and it should be noted that these three, Wyntoun, Bower, and Major, are all Scottish. John Major (or Mair) was born about 1450, and his *Historia Maioris Britanniæ* was published in 1521. In the part dealing with the reign of Richard I. (lib. iv. cap. ii.), we find:—

'About this time it was, as I conceive, that there flourished those most famous robbers Robert Hood, an Englishman, and Little John, who lay in wait in the woods, but spoiled of their goods those only who were wealthy. They took the life of no man, unless either he attacked them or offered resistance in defence of his property. Robert supported by his plundering a hundred bowmen, ready fighters every one, with whom four hundred of the strongest would not dare to engage in combat. The feats of this Robert are told in song all over Britain. He would allow no woman to suffer injustice, nor would he spoil the poor, but rather enriched them from the plunder taken from abbots. The robberies of this man I condemn, but of all thieves he was the prince and the most gentle thief.'5 This is repeated almost verbatim in Stow's *Annales* (1681).

These five references show that Robin Hood was popular in ballads for at least a century before the date at which we find those ballads in print; and apart from the fact that printing is usually the last thing that happens to a ballad of the folk, the language in which they are written is unmistakably Middle English—that is to say, the *Gest of Robyn Hode* (at least) may be dated nearer 1400 than 1500. But Langland's evidence is clear; 'rymes' of Robin Hood were widely known by 1377. Neither Bower nor Major know anything of Robin except what they learnt from the ballads about him.

II. ROBIN HOOD, EARL OF HUNTINGDON

In attempting to provide Robin Hood with a noble ancestry, Ritson quotes, amongst other authorities, a manuscript life of Robin, which, as it supplied him with other errors, had best be put out of court at once. This is Sloane MS. 780 (Ritson calls it 715, which is due to the fact that in his time Sloane MSS. 715-7, 720-1, and 780-1 were bound up together); it is of the early seventeenth century, which is much too late for any faith to be put in its statements.

No allusion to the noble descent of Robin Hood has been found earlier than one in Grafton's Chronicle (1569), where the author alleges that he takes this information from 'an olde and auncient pamphlet.' As Child says, we must 'invoke the spirit of Ritson to pardon the xviii taking of no very serious notice of Robin Hood's noble extraction.'

Stukely, an antiquary who published his *Palæographia Britannica* in 1746, derived 'Robert Fitzooth, commonly called Robin Hood, pretended Earl of Huntingdon,' from a series of Anglo-Norman lords.

It would be almost unnecessary to mention the two Elizabethan plays concerning Robert the Earl, were it not for an ingenious suggestion made in connection with them. *The Downfall of Robert Earl of Huntington*, and *The Death* of the same, were written by Anthony Munday and Henry Chettle, and are first mentioned in Henslowe's *Diary* in 1598. The Earl, being outlawed, flies to Sherwood Forest, accompanied by Matilda, daughter of Lord Fitzwater; and there he assumes the style and title of Robin Hood, and calls Matilda Maid Marian. This plot is introduced by an induction in which John Skelton the poet appears as stage-manager; and it has been suggested that Munday's play may be founded on a now-lost interlude or pageant of Skelton's composing. Robert, Lord Fitz-Walter, a descendant from the original Earls of Huntingdon, was patron of the living at Diss, in Norfolk, which Skelton held.'6

III. HISTORICAL ROBIN HOODS

In 1852 Joseph Hunter issued, as No. 4 of his 'Critical and Historical Tracts,' *The Great Hero of the ancient Minstrelsy of England, Robin Hood.* Amongst other discoveries, he found, in an Exchequer document of expenses in the royal household of Edward II., the name of 'Robyn Hode' occurring several times as a 'vadlet' or 'porteur de la chambre,' at the salary of threepence per diem, between March and November of 1324.

Various other researchers have succeeded in tracing half a dozen people, all named Robin or Robert Hood, within a period of some forty years of the fourteenth century; but few have pressed identification with Robin Hood the outlaw so far as Hunter, 'who,' says Professor Child, 'could have identified Pigrogromitus and Quinapalus, if he had given his mind to it.' Working on the above datum, Hunter shows how probable it is that Robin Hood the outlaw entered the service of Edward II. at Nottingham, where the king was from November 9-23 in 1323. But the Robin whose fortunes Hunter raked up was a very bad servant, and within a year from the alleged date was ignominiously dismissed from the king's service, with a present of 5s., 'because he was no longer able to work'! Was this the invincible champion of English yeomen? Was this the hand that launched a thousand shafts?

The only point to which attention need be called is the obvious fact that 'Robert Hood' was not an uncommon combination of names, at least in fourteenth-century England.

IV. ROBIN HOOD THE MYTH

In 1845 Adalbert Kuhn (in Haupt's *Zeitschrift*, v. 472-94) attempted to show that Robin Hood was a mythological figure representing one of the manifestations of Woden, as a vegetation deity; and half a century later Sir J. H. Ramsay suggested that he was a wood-spirit corresponding to the Hodeken of German tradition. Theories such as this[7] seem to be fascinating to all sorts of scholars, perhaps because they involve continually a minute appreciation of fine shades of probability. In the present instance they reach a point at which it is suggested that the rose-garland worn by the Potter—not in the ballad of *Robin Hood and the Potter*, but in the later play— is a survival of the Strife between xxi Summer and Winter. Certainly there is no need to seek a mythological origin for the Robin Hood of the ballads; but we must proceed to consider the Robin of folk-drama.

To do this, it is necessary to go back some centuries before the time at which we first hear of Robin Hood the outlaw, and to follow the development of the English folk's summer festival from song and dance to drama, and from the folk-games—the 'Induction of May,' the 'Induction of Autumn,' the 'Play of the King and the Queen,' which, separately or together, were performed at least as early as the thirteenth century—to the 'May-game' or 'King's game' of the middle of the fifteenth century. Going back again to the thirteenth century, and crossing over to France, we find in the *fêtes du mai*—which were evolved, with the help of the minstrels, from the French folk's summer festival—the names of Robin and Marion customarily appropriated to the king and queen of these *fêtes*.

Now between 1450 and 1500 the May-game becomes associated in England with Robin Hood: setting aside the possibility that Bower's reference, mentioned above, to 'comedies and tragedies,' may allude to the May-game, we can find many entries, in parish records from all parts of England, which show that the summer folk-festival has developed into a play of Robin Hood. Further, it has been very plausibly suggested[8] that about the same time the *French* Robin, becoming confused with the English one, brought in Marion (a French name), and thus supplied our Robin

Hood with his Maid Marian, who has no place in the true ballads of the outlaw.

In 1473 Sir John Paston wrote a letter in which he refers to a servant, of whom he says, 'I have kepyd hym this iii yer to pleye Saynt Jorge and Robyn Hod and the Shryff of Nottyngham.' There has also survived a leaf of manuscript—perhaps it is only an accident that it was formerly in the possession of the first editor of the *Paston Letters*—of about the same date, which contains a portion of the play to which Sir John refers, that of Robin Hood and the Sheriff of Nottingham,9 which is founded upon a story similar to that of the ballad of *Robin Hood and Guy of Gisborne* (see p. 128). xxiii Besides this fragment, we have in William Copland's edition of the *Gest* a dramatic appendix of 'the playe of Robyn Hoode, verye proper to be played in Maye games' (printed *c.* 1560); this in fact consists of two plays carelessly tagged together, first *Robin Hood and the Friar* (who is distinctly called Friar Tuck), and second, *Robin Hood and the Potter* (partly founded on the ballad of that name). Friar Tuck, it should be noted, occurs also in the earlier fragmentary play; but there is no friar in Robin Hood's 'meynie' in any of the older ballads, and no Maid Marian in either the older ballads or the above plays.

These complications of Robin Hood's company are further confused by the fact that the morris-dance, which was universally affiliated to the May-game, borrowed therefrom not only Maid Marian but Robin Hood, Little John and Friar Tuck; so that amongst the later ballads and broadsides we find Robin's company increased. However, by that time Robin himself had degenerated from the fine character exhibited in the earlier ballads given in this volume.

TOPOGRAPHY OF ROBIN HOOD'S HAUNTS

Although Robin Hood belongs in legend no more exclusively to any definite district than xxv his noble fore-runner King Arthur, yet, like King Arthur, he has become associated particularly with one or two haunts; and it is no easier—nor in the end more profitable—to reconcile Lyonnesse with Carlisle and Inglewood10 than to disentangle Robin Hood of Barnsdale from Robin Hood of Sherwood Forest.

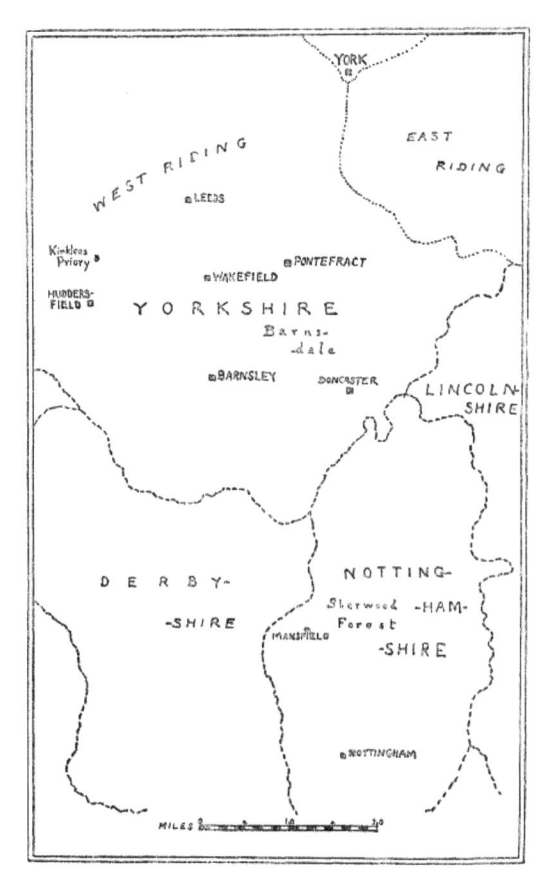

The simplest way to begin is to eliminate from our consideration the numerous Robin Hood's Hills, Wells, Stones, Oaks, or Butts, some of which may be found as far distant as Gloucestershire and Somerset; for many of these probably bear his name in much the same way as other natural freaks bear the Devil's name. A large number can be found in what may be called Robin Hood's home-counties, Yorkshire and those which touch Yorkshire—Lancashire, Derby, Nottingham and Lincoln shires.

Undoubtedly the evidence of the best ballads goes to show that at one time there must have been at least two cycles of Robin Hood ballads, one placing him in Barnsdale, the other allotting him headquarters in Sherwood; but it appears that even the ballads of the fifteenth century make little effort to discriminate between the xxvi two. *Robin Hood and the Monk* (MS. of *c.* 1450) introduces us, in its first five lovely stanzas, to Sherwood; in *Robin Hood and the Potter* (MS. of *c.* 1500), the scene is Nottingham, in the Sherwood district. Little John refers to Wentbridge, which lies in the heart of Barnsdale, yet knows every path in merry Sherwood.

In the *Gest*, compiled as it is from ballads of both cycles, no attempt was made to reconcile their various topographies; but it can be seen that the general geography of the first division of the *Gest* (Fyttes I. II. and IV.) is that of Barnsdale, while the second division (Fyttes III. V. and VI.), dealing with the Sheriff of Nottingham, mainly centres round Sherwood. In the seventh Fytte, the King goes, presumably from London (322.³), to Nottingham *via* Lancashire; and the eighth jumps from Nottingham to Kirksley.11

In *Robin Hood and Guy of Gisborne* (certainly an early ballad, although the Percy Folio, which supplies the only text, is *c.* 1650), the scene is specified as Barnsdale; yet at the end the Sheriff of Nottingham flees to his house as if it were hard by, whereas he had a fifty-mile run xxvii before him. The later ballads forget Barnsdale altogether.

BARNSDALE

The majority of the places mentioned in the northern or Barnsdale cycle will be found in the south of the West Riding of Yorkshire, a district bounded by the East Riding and Lincolnshire to the east, Derby and Nottingham shires to the south, and the river Calder to the north. To the west, the natural boundary is the high ground of the Peak, which divides Manchester from Sheffield.

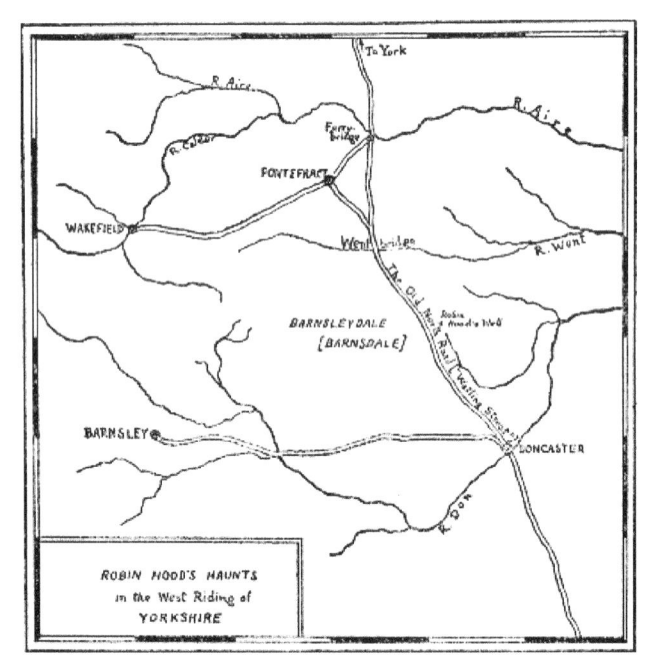

ROBIN HOOD'S HAUNTS in the West Riding of YORKSHIRE

The town of Barnsley lies slightly to the east of a line joining Leeds and Sheffield; Barnsdale itself is east and north of Barnsley, where the high backbone of the Pennines drops towards the flats surrounding the river Humber. The great North Road ('Watling Street,' *Gest*, 18.[2]) between Doncaster and Pontefract, crosses the small slow river Went at Wentbridge (probably referred to in st. 135 of the *Gest*), which may be taken as the northern boundary of Barnsdale. That this part of the North Road was considered unsafe for travellers as early as Edward I.'s reign is shown by the fact that a party going from Scotland to Winchester, and for most of the journey guarded by a dozen archers, saw fit to increase their number of guards to twenty between Pontefract and Tickhill, the latter being on the border of Yorkshire and Nottingham, south of Doncaster.

The remaining places, except those explained in the footnotes, may be dealt with here.

'Blyth' (*Gest*, 27.[4], 259.[4]), twice mentioned as a place at which to dine, is a dozen miles south of Doncaster, and in Nottingham; it is almost exactly half-way between Barnsdale and Sherwood.

'Verysdale' (*Gest*, 126.[4]) may be Wyersdale, a wild tract of the old Forest of Lancashire, near Lancaster.

'Holderness' (*Gest*, 149.[1]) is the nose of Yorkshire; between the south-easterly turn of the Humber below Hull and the North Sea.

'Kyrkesly' (*Gest*, 451.[3], 454.[3]), or 'Churchlees' (*Robin Hood's Death*, 1.[3]). Kirklees Priory is on the left or north bank of the river Calder, a few miles north of Huddersfield.

'St. Mary Abbey' is 'here besyde' (*Gest*, 54.[4]) and in York (84.[4]).

SHERWOOD

The name of Sherwood is not mentioned in the *Gest*, though that of Nottingham is frequent. The old forest was a district about twenty-five miles square, lying to the north of Nottingham, between that town and Worksop, including Mansfield and, to the north, the district now known as 'the Dukeries,' *i.e.* the parks of Welbeck, Clumber and Rufford. There is a village of Sherwood, a northern suburb of Nottingham, and a Sherwood Hall near Mansfield; between the two may be found Friar Tuck's Well, Robin Hood's Well, Robin Hood's Stable, and a Robin Hood Hill. But, as has xxx been pointed out above, these names have little significance in view of the fact that similarly-named objects can be found in other counties.

It is more interesting to note that a pasture called 'Robynhode Closse' (*i.e.* close) is mentioned in the Nottingham Chamberlain's accounts as early as 1485, and a 'Robynhode Well' in 1500.

4. So translated by Ritson. 'Comedies and tragedies' is an ambiguous phrase in the fifteenth century, and may mean either the dramatised May-games or ballads. Cf. Chambers, *Mediæval Stage*, ii. 211.

5. Translation (except the last phrase) by A. Constable, Edinburgh, 1892.

6. See H. L. D. Ward's *Catalogue of Romances*, 506, under the Romance of Fulk Fitz-Warine.

7. The suggestion that 'Hood' = 'o' Wood' was originally made in the *Gentleman's Magazine* for March 1793, over the signature D. H.

8. First, as regards Marian, by Warton, *History of English Poetry* (1774), p. 245: recently and in more detail by E. K. Chambers, *Mediæval Stage* (1903), i. 176.

9. This leaf has lately been given to the Library of Trinity College, Cambridge, by Mr. Aldis Wright. It may be seen in facsimile as well as in type in the *Collections* (p. 117) of the Malone Society (Part ii., 1908), where the two plays of Robin Hood mentioned above are also reprinted.

10. It should be remembered that Wyntoun says that Robin Hood plied his trade in Inglewood and Barnsdale (see ante, p. xiv.).

11. Child, in saying that 'Robin Hood has made a vow to go from London to Barnsdale' (v. 51) seems to assume that the 'king's court' (*Gest*, 433) implies London, which, however, is not specified.

SHORT BIBLIOGRAPHY OF ROBIN HOOD

RITSON, Joseph. Robin Hood: A Collection of all the ancient Poems, Songs, and Ballads, now extant, relative to that celebrated English Outlaw. 2 vols. London, 1795.

GUTCH, John Matthew. A Lytell Geste of Robin Hode, with other Ancient and Modern Ballads and Songs relating to this celebrated yeoman. 2 vols. London, 1847.

HUNTER, Rev. Joseph. The Ballad-Hero Robin Hood. London, 1852. (No. of *Critical and Historical Tracts*.)

FRICKE, Richard. Die Robin-Hood-Balladen. In Herrig's *Archiv*, lxix. 241-344. Also separately, Braunschweig, 1883.

BRANDL, Alois. Englische Volkspoesie. In Paul's *Grundriss der Germanischen Philologie*. Strassburg, 1893.

KIESSMAN, R. Untersuchungen über die Motivs der Robin-Hood-Balladen. Halle, 1895.

CHAMBERS, E. K. The Mediæval Stage. 2 vols. Oxford, 1903. (Vol. i, chap. viii.)

HEUSLER, A. Lied und Epos. Dortmund, 1905.

HART, W. M. Ballad and Epic. In *Harvard Studies and Notes in Philology and Literature*. Vol. xi. Boston, 1907.

CLAWSON, W. H. The Gest of Robin Hood. In *University of Toronto Studies*. Toronto, 1909.

ARTICLES

The London and Westminster Review. March 1840. Vol. xxxiii.

The Academy (correspondence). 1883. Vol. xxiv.

The Quarterly Review. July 1898.

A GEST OF ROBYN HODE

'Rebus huius Roberti gestis tota Britannia in cantibus utitur.'

Major.

THE TEXT.—There are seven texts of the *Gest*, to be distinguished as follows:—

(i.) begins 'Here begynneth a gest of Robyn Hode'; an undated printed fragment preserved with other early pieces in a volume in the Advocates' Library, Edinburgh. It was reprinted in 1827 by David Laing, who then supposed it to be from the press of Chepman and Myllar, Edinburgh printers of the early sixteenth century; but he afterwards had reason to doubt this opinion. It is now attributed to Jan van Doesborch, a printer from Antwerp. The extent of this fragment is indicated below. Internal evidence (collected by Child, iii. 40) shows it to be an older text than

(ii.) 'Here begynneth a lytell geste of Robyn hode'—so runs the title-page; at the head of the poem are added the words—'and his meyne [= meinie, company], And of the proude Sheryfe of Notyngham.' The colophon runs 'Explycit. kynge Edwarde and Robyn hode and Lytell Johan Enprented at London in fletestrete at the sygne of the sone By Wynken de Worde.' This also is undated, and Child says it 'may be anywhere from 1492 to 1534.' Recent bibliographical research shows that Wynkyn de Worde moved to Fleet Street at the end of the year 1500, which gives the downward limit; and as the printer died in 1584, the *Lytell Geste* must be placed between those dates.1 The text is complete save for two lines (7.¹ and 339.¹), which have also dropped from the other early texts. The only known copy is in the Cambridge University Library.

(iii., iv. and v.) Three mutilated printed fragments, containing about thirty-five, seventy, and fifteen stanzas respectively, preserved amongst the Douce fragments in the Bodleian (the last presented by J. O. Halliwell-Phillipps). The first was lent to Ritson in or before 1790 by Farmer, who thought it to be Rastell's printing; in Ritson's second edition (1836) he says he gave it to Douce, and states without reason that it is of de Worde's printing 'probably in 1489.'

(vi.) *A mery geste of Robyn Hoode*, etc., a quarto preserved in the British Museum, not dated, but printed 'at London vpon the thre Crane wharfe by wyllyam Copland,' who printed there about 1560. This edition also contains 'a newe playe for to be played in Maye games, very plesaunte and full of pastyme.'

(vii.) *A Merry Iest of Robin Hood*, etc., printed at London for Edward White; no date, but perhaps the 'pastorall plesant commedie' entered to White in the Stationers' Registers, May 14, 1594. There is a copy of this in the Bodleian, and another was in the Huth Library.

THE TEXT here given is mainly the Wynkyn de Worde text, except where the earlier Edinburgh fragment is available; the stanzas which the latter preserves are here numbered 1.-83.[3], 113.[4]-124.[1], 127.[4]-133.[2], 136.[4]-208.[3], and 314.[2]-349.[3], omitting 2.[2,3] and 3 7.[1]. A few variations are recorded in the footnotes, it being unnecessary in the present edition to do more than refer to Child's laborious collation of all the above texts.

The spelling of the old texts is retained with very few exceptions. The reason for this is that although the original texts were printed in the sixteenth century, the language is of the fifteenth, and a number of Middle English forms remain; these are pointed out by Child, iii. 40, and elaborately classified by W. H. Clawson, *The Gest of Robin Hood*, 4-5. A possible alternative was to treat the *Gest* on the plan adopted for fifteenth-century texts by E. K. Chambers and the present editor in *Early English Lyrics* (1907); but in that book the editors were mostly concerned with texts printed from manuscript, whereas here there is good reason to suspect the existence of a text or texts previous to those now available. For the sounded e (ë) I have mostly followed Child.

The *Gest* is not a single ballad, but a conglomeration of several, forming a short epic. Ballads representing its component parts are not now extant; although on the other hand there are later ballads founded on certain episodes in the *Gest*. The compiler availed himself of incidents from other traditional sources, but he produced a singularly original tale.

The word *gest*, now almost obsolete, is derived through Old French from the Latin *gesta*, 'deeds' or 'exploits.' But as the word was particularly applied to 'exploits as narrated or recited,' there came into use a secondary meaning—that of 'a story or romantic tale in verse,' or 'a metrical chronicle.' The latter meaning is doubtless intended in the title of the *Gest of Robyn Hode*. A further corruption may be noticed even in the titles of the later texts as given above; Copland adds the word 'mery,' which thirty years later causes White to print a 'Merry Jest.'

I have kept the original divisions of the story into eight 'fyttes,' but it falls more naturally into three main sections, in each of which a complete story is narrated. These may he distinguished thus:—

1. ROBIN HOOD AND THE KNIGHT.
(Fyttes First, Second, and Fourth.)

2. ROBIN HOOD, LITTLE JOHN, AND THE SHERIFF OF NOTTINGHAM.
(Fyttes Third, Fifth, and Sixth.)

3. ROBIN HOOD AND KING EDWARD.
(Fyttes Seventh and Eighth.)

An argument and general notes are prefixed to each fytte.

THE FIRST FYTTE (1-81)

ARGUMENT.—Robin Hood refuses to dine until he finds some guest to provide money for his entertainment. He sends Little John and all his men to bring in any earl, baron, abbot, or knight, to dine with him. They find a knight, and feast him beneath the greenwood tree: but when Robin demands payment, the knight turns out to be in sorry plight, for he has sold all his goods to save his son. On the security of Our Lady, Robin lends him four hundred pounds, and gives him a livery, a horse, a palfrey, boots, spurs, etc., and Little John as squire.

Robin's unwillingness to dine until he has a guest appears to be a parody of King Arthur's custom of refusing dinner until he has had an adventure. (See Child, i. 257, note ‡.) The offer of the Virgin as security for a loan is apparently derived from a well-known miracle of Mary, in which a Christian, wishing to borrow money of a Jew, takes him to a church and makes him lay his hand on a statue of the Virgin and Child, praying that, if he fails to return the money on the day fixed to the lender, but gives it to the statue, Christ will return it to the Jew. This miracle eventually takes place, but is attributed rather to the Virgin than to her Son. (See Child, iii. 52.)

1. Mr. Charles Sayle puts it 'before 1519' in his catalogue of the early printed books in the University Library.

THE FIRST FYTTE

    1.

    1.[1] 'Lythe and listin,' hearken and listen: a very common opening.

    1.[2] 'frebore,' free-born.

    LYTHE and listin, gentilmen,

    That be of frebore blode;

    I shall you tel of a gode yeman,

    His name was Robyn Hode.

    2.

    2.[2,3] 'Whyles . . . outlaw': supplied from the Wynkyn de Worde text.

    Robyn was a prude outlaw,

Whyles he walked on grounde;

So curteyse an outlaw as he was one

Was never non yfounde.

3.

Robyn stode in Bernesdale,

And lenyd hym to a tre;

And bi him stode Litell Johnn,

A gode yeman was he.

4.

4.[4] *i.e.*, worthy of a groom, or young man.

And alsoo dyd gode Scarlok,

And Much, the miller's son;

There was none ynch of his bodi

But it was worth a grome.

5.

5.[3] 'and,' if.

Than bespake Lytell Johnn

All untoo Robyn Hode:

'Maister, and ye wolde dyne betyme

It wolde doo you moche gode.'

6.

6.[4] 'unkouth,' unknown.

Than bespake hym gode Robyn:

'To dyne have I noo lust,

Till that I have som bolde baron,

Or som unkouth gest.

7.

7.[1] Wanting in all versions.

7.[3] 'som,' supplied from Wynken de Worde's text.

.   .   .   .   .

'That may pay for the best,
Or some knyght or som squyer
That dwelleth here bi west.'

8.

8.[4] 'messis,' masses.

A gode maner than had Robyn:
In londe where that he were,
Every day or he wold dyne
Thre messis wolde he here.

9.

9.[4] 'allther moste,' most of all.

The one in the worship of the Fader,
And another of the Holy Gost,
The thirde was of Our dere Lady
That he loved allther moste.

10.

10.[2] 'dout,' fear.

Robyn loved Oure dere Lady;
For dout of dydly synne,
Wolde he never do compani harme
That any woman was in.

11.

'Maistar,' than sayde Lytil Johnn,
'And we our borde shal sprede,
Tell us wheeler that we shall go
And what life that we shall lede.

12.

12.³ 'reve,' pillage.

'Where we shall take, where we shall leve,

Where we shall abide behynde;

Where we shall robbe, where we shall reve,

Where we shall bete and bynde.'

13.

13.¹ 'no force,' no matter.

'Thereof no force,' than sayde Robyn;

'We shall do well inowe;

But loke ye do no husbonde harme

That tilleth with his ploughe.

14.

'No more ye shall no gode yeman

That walketh by grene-wode shawe;

Ne no knyght ne no squyer

That wol be a gode felawe.

15.

'These bisshoppes and these archebisshoppes,

Ye shall them bete and bynde;

The hye sherif of Notyingham,

Hym holde ye in your mynde.'

16.

16.² 'lere,' learn.

16.³ 'fer dayes,' late in the day: 'gest,' exploit.

'This worde shalbe holde,' sayde Lytell Johnn,

'And this lesson we shall lere;

It is fer dayes; God sende us a gest,

That we were at our dynere.'

17.

'Take thy gode bowe in thy honde,' sayde Robyn;

'Late Much wende with thee;

And so shal Willyam Scarlok,

And no man abyde with me.

18.

18.[1] The Sayles, a small part of the manor of Pontefract.

18.[2] Watling Street = the great North Road.

18.[4] 'Up chaunce,' in case.

'And walke up to the Saylis

And so to Watlinge Strete,

And wayte after some unkuth gest,

Up chaunce ye may them mete.

19.

19.[4] 'dight,' prepared.

'Be he erle, or ani baron,

Abbot, or ani knyght,

Bringhe hym to lodge to me;

His dyner shall be dight.'

20.

They wente up to the Saylis,

These yemen all three;

They loked est, they loked weest,

They myght no man see.

21.

21.[2] 'dernë strete,' hidden or obscure path.

But as they loked in to Bernysdale,

Bi a dernë strete,

Than came a knyght ridinghe;
Full sone they gan hym mete.
22.
All dreri was his semblaunce,
And lytell was his pryde;
His one fote in the styrop stode,
That othere wavyd beside.
23.
23.[1] 'iyn,' eyes.
His hode hanged in his iyn two;
He rode in symple aray;
A soriar man than he was one
Rode never in somer day.
24.
Litell Johnn was full curteyes,
And sette hym on his kne:
'Welcome be ye, gentyll knyght,
Welcom ar ye to me.
25.
25.[2] 'Hendë,' noble.
'Welcom be thou to grenë wode,
Hendë knyght and fre;
My maister hath abiden you fastinge,
Syr, al these ourës thre.'
26.
'Who is thy maister?' sayde the knyght;
Johnn sayde, 'Robyn Hode';
'He is a gode yoman,' sayde the knyght,
'Of hym I have herde moche gode.

27.

27.² 'in fere,' in company.

'I graunte,' he sayde, 'with you to wende,

My bretherne, all in fere;

My purpos was to have dyned to day

At Blith or Dancastere.'

28.

28.² 'carefull chere,' sorrowful face.

28.⁴ 'lere,' cheek.

Furth than went this gentyl knight,

With a carefull chere;

The teris oute of his iyen ran,

And fell downe by his lere.

29.

They brought him to the lodgë-dore;

Whan Robyn gan hym see,

Full curtesly dyd of his hode

And sette hym on his knee.

30.

'Welcome, sir knight,' than sayde Robyn,

'Welcome art thou to me;

I have abyden you fastinge, sir,

All these ouris thre.'

31.

31.⁴ 'meynë,' company.

Than answered the gentyll knight,

With wordës fayre and fre:

'God thee save, goode Robyn,

And all thy fayre meynë.'

32.

32.⁴ 'noumbles,' entrails.

They wasshed togeder and wyped bothe,

And sette to theyr dynere;

Brede and wyne they had right ynoughe,

And noumbles of the dere.

33.

Swannes and fessauntes they had full gode,

And foules of the ryvere;

There fayled none so litell a birde

That ever was bred on bryre.

34.

34.¹ 'Do gladly' = make yourself at home; a hospitable expression. Cp. 103.¹ and 232.¹.

'Do gladly, sir knight,' sayde Robyn;

'Gramarcy, sir,' sayde he;

'Suche a dinere had I nat

Of all these wekys thre.

35.

'If I come ageyne, Robyn,

Here by thys contrë,

As gode a dyner I shall thee make

As thou haest made to me.'

36.

'Gramarcy, knyght,' sayde Robyn;

'My dyner whan that I it have,

I was never so gredy, by dere worthy God,

My dyner for to crave.

37.

37.¹ 'or ye wende,' before you go.

'But pay or ye wende,' sayde Robyn;

'Me thynketh it is gode ryght;

It was never the maner, by dere worthi God,

A yoman to pay for a knyght.'

38.

38.4 'let not,' leave nothing undone.

'I have nought in my coffers,' saide the knyght,

'That I may prefer for shame':

'Litell John, go loke,' sayde Robyn,

'Ne let not for no blame.

39.

39.2,4 'have parte of,' perhaps means 'protect,' or 'take my part.'

'Tel me truth,' than saide Robyn,

'So God have parte of thee':

'I have no more but ten shelynges,' sayde the knyght,

'So God have parte of me.'

40.

'If thou have no more,' sayde Robyn,

'I woll nat one peny;

And yf thou have nede of any more,

More shall I lend the.

41.

'Go nowe furth, Littell Johnn,

The truth tell thou me;

If there be no more but ten shelinges,

No peny that I se.'

42.

Lyttell Johnn sprede downe hys mantell

Full fayre upon the grounde,

And there he fonde in the knyghtës cofer

But even halfe a pounde.

43.

Littell Johnn let it lye full styll,

And went to hys maysteer full lowe;

'What tydynges, Johnn?' sayde Robyn;

'Sir, the knyght is true inowe.'

44.

'Fyll of the best wine,' sayde Robyn,

'The knyght shall begynne;

Moche wonder thinketh me

Thy clothynge is so thinne.

45.

45.[3] This refers to 'distraint of knighthood,' instituted in 1224, compelling military tenants to receive knighthood or pay a composition.

'Tell me one worde,' sayde Robyn,

'And counsel shal it be;

I trowe thou wert made a knyght of force,

Or ellys of yemanry.

46.

46.[3] 'okerer,' usurer.

'Or ellys thou hast been a sori husbande,

And lyved in stroke and strife;

An okerer, or ellis a lechoure,' sayde Robyn,

'Wyth wronge hast led thy lyfe.'

47.

'I am none of those,' sayde the knyght,

'By God that madë me;

An hundred wynter here before

Myn auncetres knyghtes have be.

48.

48.² 'disgrate,' unfortunate.

'But oft it hath befal, Robyn,

A man hath be disgrate;

But God that sitteth in heven above

May amende his state.

49.

49.⁴ From the rhyme it is obvious the verses have here been confused, especially as all copies print 50.³ before 50.².

'Withyn this two yere, Robyne,' he sayde,

'My neghbours well it knowe,

Foure hundred pounde of gode money

Ful well than myght I spende.

50.

'Nowe have I no gode,' saide the knyght,

'God hath shapen suche an ende,

But my chyldren and my wyfe,

Tyll God yt may amende.'

51.

'In what maner,' than sayde Robyn,

'Hast thou lorne thy rychesse?'

'For my greate foly,' he sayde,

'And for my kyndënesse.

52.

52.⁴ 'just,' joust, tilt.

'I hade a sone, forsoth, Robyn,

That shulde have ben myn ayre,

Whanne he was twenty wynter olde,

In felde wolde just full fayre.

53.

53.⁴, 54.¹ 'beth' (in another version 'both'), are.

'He slewe a knyght of Lancashire,

And a squyer bolde;

For to save him in his ryght

My godes beth sette and solde.

54.

54.¹ 'sette to wedde,' put in pledge.

'My londes beth sette to wedde, Robyn,

Untyll a certayn day,

To a ryche abbot here besyde

Of Seynt Mari Abbey.'

55.

'What is the som?' sayde Robyn;

'Trouth than tell thou me.'

'Sir,' he sayde, 'foure hundred pounde;

The abbot told it to me.'

56.

56.¹ 'lese,' lose.

'Nowe and thou lese thy lond,' sayde Robyn,

'What shall fall of thee?'

'Hastely I wol me buske,' sayd the knyght,

'Over the saltë see,

57.

57.¹ 'quyke' = quick, alive.

'And se where Criste was quyke and dede,

On the mount of Calverë;

Fare wel, frende, and have gode day;

It may no better be.'

58.

Teris fell out of hys iyen two;

He wolde have gone hys way;

'Farewel, frende, and have gode day,

I ne have no more to pay.'

59.

59.[4] 'blowe,' utter.

'Where be thy frendës?' sayde Robyn:

'Syr, never one wol me knowe;

While I was rych ynowe at home

Great boste than wolde they blowe.

60.

60.[2] 'on a rowe,' in file.

'And nowe they renne away fro me,

As bestis on a rowe;

They take no more hede of me

Thanne they had me never sawe.'

61.

61.[1] 'ruthe,' pity.

61.[4] 'chere,' entertainment.

For ruthe thanne wept Litell Johnn,

Scarlok and Much in fere;

'Fyl of the best wyne,' sayde Robyn,

'For here is a symple chere.

62.

62.[2] 'borrowe,' security.

'Hast thou any frende,' sayde Robyn,

'Thy borrowe that woldë be?'

'I have none,' than sayde the knyght,

'But God that dyed on tree.'

63.

'Do away thy japis,' than sayde Robyn,

'Thereof wol I right none;

Wenest thou I wolde have God to borowe,

Peter, Poule, or Johnn?

64.

64.² 'shope,' shaped.

'Nay, by hym that me made,

And shope both sonne and mone,

Fynde me a better borowe,' sayde Robyn,

'Or money getest thou none.'

65.

65.⁴ 'or,' before.

'I have none other,' sayde the knyght,

'The sothe for to say,

But yf yt be Our dere Lady;

She fayled me never or thys day.'

66.

66.³ 'pay,' liking.

'By dere worthy God,' sayde Robyn,

'To seche all Englonde thorowe,

Yet fonde I never to my pay

A moche better borowe.

67.

'Come nowe furth, Litell Johnn,

And go to my tresourë,

And bringe me foure hundred pound,

And loke well tolde it be.'

68.

Furth than went Litell Johnn,

And Scarlok went before;

He tolde oute foure hundred pounde

By eight and twenty score.

69.

'Is thys well tolde?' sayde lytell Much;

Johnn sayde: 'What greveth thee?

It is almus to helpe a gentyll knyght

That is fal in povertë.

70.

'Master,' than sayde Lityll John,

'His clothinge is full thynne;

Ye must gyve the knight a lyveray,

To lappe his body therein.

71.

'For ye have scarlet and grene, mayster,

And many a rich aray;

Ther is no marchaunt in mery Englond

So ryche, I dare well say.'

72.

72.[2] 'mete,' measured. So 73.[1] 'met' = measured.

'Take hym thre yerdes of every colour,

And loke well mete that it be.'

Lytell Johnn toke none other mesure

But his bowë-tree.

73.

And at every handfull that he met

He lepëd fotës three;

'What devylles drapar,' sayd litell Much,
'Thynkest thou for to be?'

74.

74.¹ 'loughe,' laughed.

Scarlok stode full stil and loughe,
And sayd, 'By God Almyght,
Johnn may gyve hym gode mesure,
For it costeth hym but lyght.'

75.

'Mayster,' than said Litell Johnn
To gentill Robyn Hode,
'Ye must give the knight a hors
To lede home al this gode.'

76.

'Take him a gray coursar,' sayde Robyn,
'And a saydle newe;
He is Oure Ladye's messangere;
God graunt that he be true.'

77.

'And a gode palfray,' sayde lytell Much,
'To mayntene hym in his right';
'And a peyre of botës,' sayde Scarlok,
'For he is a gentyll knight.'

78.

78.⁴ 'tene,' trouble.

'What shalt thou gyve him, Litell John?'
'Sir, a peyre of gilt sporis clene,
To pray for all this company;

God bringe hym oute of tene.'

79.

'Whan shal mi day be,' said the knight,

'Sir, and your wyll be?'

'This day twelve moneth,' saide Robyn,

'Under this grene-wode tre.

80.

'It were great shamë,' said Robyn,

'A knight alone to ryde,

Withoutë squyre, yoman, or page,

To walkë by his syde.

81.

81.[2] 'knave,' servant.

81.[3] *i.e.*, he shall stand for thee instead of a yeoman.

'I shal thee lende Litell Johnn, my man,

For he shalbe thy knave;

In a yeman's stede he may thee stande,

If thou greate nedë have.'

THE SECOND FYTTE (82-143)

ARGUMENT.—The knight goes to York to pay down his four hundred pounds to the abbot of St. Mary Abbey, who has retained the services of the high justice of England 'with cloth and fee,' an offence defined as conspiracy by statutes of the first three Edwards (see *Notes and Queries*, First Series, vol. vi. p. 479). The knight, pretending he has not brought the money, requests an extension of time; but the abbot will not hear of it, and is supported in his refusal by the justice: the knight's lands will be forfeited. The justice advises the abbot (117, etc.) to give the knight a sum to 'make a release' and prevent subsequent legal difficulties. The knight brings the matter to an end by paying down the four hundred pounds, saying that had the abbot been more courteous, he should have had interest on the loan.

The knight returns to his home in Wyresdale, and saves up the sum to be repaid to Robin Hood. As he sets out for Barnsdale with a goodly company, he finds a great wrestling-match taking place at Wentbridge,[2] which delays him a while.

The word 'frembde' (138.[3]) is now obsolete except in Scots and north-country dialect, and is spelled in various ways. It occurs more than once in Chaucer, and twice in Sidney's *Arcadia*. 'Fremit,' the common Scots form, may be found in Burns. More recently, it appears in books of Westmoreland, Cumberland, or Northumberland dialect. Cp. Mrs. Gaskell, *Sylvia's Lovers*: 'There's a fremd man i' t' house.' It means 'foreign' or 'strange.'

[2.] Wentbridge is mentioned in *Robin Hood and the Potter*, 6.[1]. The river Went is the northern boundary of Barnsdale.

THE SECOND FYTTE

82.

NOW is the knight gone on his way;

This game hym thought full gode;

Whanne he loked on Bernësdale

He blessyd Robyn Hode.

83.

83.[4] From here to 118.[3] the Edinburgh fragment is wanting.

And whanne he thought on Bernysdale,

On Scarlok, Much and Johnn

He blyssyd them for the best company

That ever he in come.

84.

Then spake that gentyll knyght,

To Lytel Johan gan he saye,

'To-morrowe I must to Yorke toune,

To Saynt Mary abbay.

85.

'And to the abbot of that place

Foure hondred pounde I must pay;

And but I be there upon this nyght

My londe is lost for ay.'

86.

86.[1] 'covent' = convent.

The abbot sayd to his covent,

There he stode on grounde,

'This day twelfe moneth came there a knyght

And borowed foure hondred pounde.

87.

87.[1] Wanting: supplied by Ritson.

87.[3] 'But,' unless: 'ylkë,' same.

[He borowed four hondred pounde]

Upon all his londë fre;

But he come this ylkë day

Disherited shall he be.'

88.

88.[3] 'lever,' rather.

'It is full erely,' sayd the pryoure,

The day is not yet ferre gone;

I had lever to pay an hondred pounde,

And lay downe anone.

89.

'The knyght is ferre beyonde the see,

In Englonde is his ryght,

And suffreth honger and colde

And many a sory nyght.

90.

'It were grete pytë,' said the pryoure,

'So to have his londe;

And ye be so lyght of your consyence,

Ye do to hym moch wronge.'

91.

91.[4] 'selerer' cellarer or steward.

'Thou arte ever in my berde,' sayd the abbot,

'By God and Saynt Rycharde';

With that cam in a fat-heded monke,

The heygh selerer.

92.

92.[2] 'bought,' ransomed.

'He is dede or hanged,' sayd the monke,

'By God that bought me dere,

And we shall have to spende in this place

Foure hondred pounde by yere.'

93.

93.[3] 'highe,' supplied from Copland's edition.

The abbot and the hy selerer

Stertë forthe full bolde,

The highe justyce of Englonde
The abbot there dyde holde.

94.

The hye justyce and many mo
Had take in to theyr honde
Holy all the knyghtës det,
To put that knyght to wronge.

95.

95.¹ 'demed,' judged.

95.⁴ 'dysheryte,' dispossessed; cf. 87.⁴.

They demed the knyght wonder sore,
The abbot and his meynë:
'But he come this ylkë day
Dysheryte shall he be.'

96.

'He wyll not come yet,' sayd the justyce,
'I dare well undertake';
But in sorowe tymë for them all
The knight came to the gate.

97.

Than bespake that gentyll knyght
Untyll his meynë:
'Now put on your symple wedes
That ye brought fro the see.'

98.

98. Wanting in all editions: supplied by Ritson.

[They put on their symple wedes,]
They came to the gates anone;
The porter was redy hymselfe

And welcomed them everychone.

99.

'Welcome, syr knyght,' sayd the porter,

'My lorde to mete is he,

And so is many a gentyll man,

For the love of thee.'

100.

100.³ 'coresed,' perhaps = coursed; *i.e.* a horse used in tourneys, a courser, or charger.

The porter swore a full grete othe:

'By God that madë me,

Here be the best coresed hors

That ever yet sawe I me.

101.

'Lede them in to the stable,' he sayd,

'That eased myght they be';

'They shall not come therin,' sayd the knyght,

'By God that dyed on a tre.'

102.

102.⁴ 'salved,' greeted.

Lordës were to mete isette

In that abbotes hall;

The knyght went forth and kneled down,

And salved them grete and small.

103.

103.¹ See 34.¹.

'Do gladly, syr abbot,' sayd the knyght,

'I am come to holde my day.'

The fyrst word that the abbot spake,

'Hast thou brought my pay?'

104.

104.[3] 'shrewed,' cursed.

'Not one peny,' sayd the knyght,

'By God that makëd me.'

'Thou art a shrewed dettour,' sayd the abbot;

'Syr justyce, drynke to me.

105.

105.[2] 'But,' unless. So 111.[3]

'What doost thou here,' sayd the abbot,

'But thou haddest brought thy pay?'

'For God,' than sayd the knyght,

'To pray of a lenger daye.'

106.

106.[4] 'fone,' foes.

'Thy daye is broke,' sayd the justyce,

'Londë getest thou none.'

'Now, good syr justyce, be my frende

And fende me of my fone!'

107.

107.[1,2] 'retained by presents of cloth and money.' —CHILD.

'I am holde with the abbot,' sayd the justyce,

'Both with cloth and fee.'

'Now, good syr sheryf, be my frende!'

'Nay, for God,' sayd he.

108.

108.[4] 'made the gree,' paid my dues. (Old French *gre*, Latin *gratum*.)

'Now, good syr abbot, be my frende,

For thy curteysë,

And holde my londës in thy honde

Tyll I have made the gree!

109.

'And I wyll be thy true servaunte,

And trewely serve the,

Tyll ye have foure hondred pounde

Of money good and free.'

110.

The abbot sware a full grete othe,

'By God that dyed on a tree,

Get the londë where thou may,

For thou getest none of me.'

111.

'By dere worthy God,' then sayd the knyght,

'That all this worldë wrought,

But I have my londe agayne,

Full dere it shall be bought.

112.

112.2 'Leve,' grant.

112.4 'Or that,' before that. The proverb is a favourite in Middle English: see *Early English Lyrics*, CXI.

'God, that was of a mayden borne,

Leve us well to spede!

For it is good to assay a frende

Or that a man have nede.'

113.

The abbot lothely on hym gan loke,

And vylaynesly hym gan call;

'Out,' he sayd, 'thou false knyght,

Spede thee out of my hall!'

114.

'Thou lyest,' then sayd the gentyll knyght,

'Abbot, in thy hal;

False knyght was I never,

By God that made us all.'

115.

Up then stode that gentyll knyght,

To the abbot sayd he,

'To suffre a knyght to knele so longe,

Thou canst no curteysye.

116.

116.³ 'as ferre in prees,' in as thick a part of the fight.

'In joustës and in tournement

Full ferre than have I be,

And put myself as ferre in prees

As ony that ever I se.'

117.

'What wyll ye gyve more,' sayd the justyce,

'And the knyght shall make a releyse?

And ellës dare I safly swere

Ye holde never your londe in pees.'

118.

118.⁴ From here to 124.¹ the Edinburgh fragment is available.

'An hondred pounde,' sayd the abbot;

The justice sayd, 'Gyve hym two';

'Nay, be God,' sayd the knyght,

'Yit gete ye it not so.

119.

119.² 'nere,' nearer. Cp. *Robin Hood and the Potter*, 46.³.

'Though ye wolde gyve a thousand more,

Yet were ye never the nere;

Shal there never be myn heyre

Abbot, justice, ne frere.'

120.

He stert hym to a borde anone,

Tyll a table rounde,

And there he shoke oute of a bagge

Even four hundred pound.

121.

'Have here thi golde, sir abbot,' saide the knight,

'Which that thou lentest me;

Had thou ben curtes at my comynge,

Rewarded shuldest thou have be.'

122.

The abbot sat styll, and ete no more,

For all his ryall fare;

He cast his hede on his shulder,

And fast began to stare.

123.

123.² 'toke,' gave.

'Take me my golde agayne,' saide the abbot,

'Sir justice, that I toke thee.'

'Not a peni,' said the justice,

'Bi God, that dyed on tree.'

124.

'Sir abbot, and ye men of lawe,

Now have I holde my daye:

Now shall I have my londe agayne,

For ought that you can saye.'

125.

The knyght stert out of the dore,

Awaye was all his care,

And on he put his good clothynge,

The other he lefte there.

126.

126.⁴ 'Verysdale,' Wyresdale or Wyersdale.

He wente hym forth full mery syngynge,

As men have tolde in tale;

His lady met hym at the gate,

At home in Verysdale.

127.

127.⁴ The Edinburgh fragment is again available as far as 133.².

'Welcome, my lorde,' sayd his lady;

'Syr, lost is all your good?'

'Be mery, dame,' sayd the knyght,

'And pray for Robyn Hode,

128.

128.² 'tene,' trouble.

'That ever his soulë be in blysse:

He holpe me out of tene;

Ne had be his kyndënesse,

Beggers had we bene.

129.

'The abbot and I accorded ben,

He is served of his pay;

The god yoman lent it me

As I cam by the way.'

130.

This knight than dwelled fayre at home,

The sothë for to saye,

Tyll he had gete four hundred pound,

Al redy for to pay.

131.

131.² 'ydyght,' fitted.

He purveyed him an hundred bowes,

The stryngës well ydyght,

An hundred shefe of arowes gode,

The hedys burneshed full bryght;

132.

132.³ 'Inocked' = i-nocked, notched.

And every arowe an ellë longe,

With pecok well idyght,

Inocked all with whyte silver;

It was a semely syght.

133.

133.¹,² The latter halves of these lines are torn away in the Edinburgh fragment. The Cambridge text is resumed at 133.³.

133.² 'stede,' place.

He purveyed him an hondreth men,

Well harnessed in that stede,

And hym selfe in that same sete,

And clothed in whyte and rede.

134.

134.¹ 'launsgay,' javelin.

134.² 'male,' baggage. Cp. 374.¹.

He bare a launsgay in his honde,

And a man ledde his male,

And reden with a lyght songe

Unto Bernysdale.

135.

135.[1] So the Cambridge text: Child suggests '? But at Wentbrydge ther was.' See Argument.

But as he went at a brydge ther was a wrastelyng,

And there taryed was he,

And there was all the best yemen

Of all the west countree.

136.

136.[2] 'i-pyght,' put.

136.[4] Edinburgh fragment again.

A full fayre game there was up set,

A whyte bulle up i-pyght,

A grete courser, with sadle and brydil,

With golde burnyssht full bryght.

137.

A payre of gloves, a rede golde rynge,

A pype of wyne, in fay;

What man that bereth hym best i-wys

The pryce shall bere away.

138.

138.[3] 'frembde bested,' in the position of a foreigner or stranger. See fore-note.

There was a yoman in that place,

And best worthy was he,

And for he was ferre and frembde bested,

Slayne he shulde have be.

139.

The knight had ruthe of this yoman,

In placë where that he stode;

He sayde that yoman shulde have no harme,

For love of Robyn Hode.

140.

140.² 'free,' supplied from the 'fere,' misprinted in the Cambridge text. Copland, 'in fere.'

140.⁴ 'shende,' put to rout.

The knyght presed in to the place,

An hundreth folowed hym [free],

With bowes bent and arowes sharpe,

For to shende that companye.

141.

141.¹ 'rome,' room.

They shulderd all and made hym rome,

To wete what he wolde say;

He took the yeman bi the hande,

And gave hym al the play.

142.

He gave hym five marke for his wyne,

There it lay on the molde,

And bad it shulde be set a broche,

Drynkë who so wolde.

143.

Thus longe taried this gentyll knyght,

Tyll that play was done;

So long abode Robyn fastinge

Thre hourës after the none.

THE THIRD FYTTE (144-204)

ARGUMENT.—The narrative of the knight's loan is for the moment dropped, in order to relate a gest of Little John, who is now (81.[2]) the knight's 'knave' or squire. Going forth 'upon a mery day,' Little John shoots with such skill that he attracts the attention of the Sheriff of Nottingham (who is here and elsewhere the type of Robin Hood's enemies), and enters his service for a year under the name of Reynold Greenleaf. While the sheriff is hunting, Little John fights his servants, robs his treasure-house, and escapes back to Robin Hood with 'three hundred pound and more.' He then bethinks him of a shrewd wile, and inveigles the sheriff to leave his hunting in order to see a right fair hart and seven score of deer, which turn out to be Robin and his men. Robin Hood exacts an oath of the sheriff, equivalent to an armistice; and he returns home, having had his fill of the greenwood.

THE THIRD FYTTE

144.

LYTH and lystyn, gentilmen,

All that now be here;

Of Litell Johnn, that was the knightës man,

Goode myrth ye shall here.

145.

145.[2] 'shete,' shoot.

145.[3] 'fet,' fetched.

It was upon a mery day

That yonge men wolde go shete;

Lytell Johnn fet his bowe anone,

And sayde he wolde them mete.

146.

Thre tymes Litell Johnn shet aboute,

And alwey he slet the wande;

The proudë sherif of Notingham

By the markës can stande.

147.

The sherif swore a full greate othe:

'By hym that dyede on a tre,

This man is the best arschere

That ever yet sawe I me.

148.

148.¹ 'wight,' strong, active.

148.⁴ 'wonynge wane': both words mean dwelling or habitation.

'Say me nowe, wight yonge man,

What is nowe thy name?

In what countrë were thou borne,

And where is thy wonynge wane?'

149.

'In Holdernes, sir, I was borne,

I-wys al of my dame;

Men cal me Reynolde Grenëlef

Whan I am at home.'

150.

'Sey me, Reynolde Grenëlefe,

Wolde thou dwell with me?

And every yere I woll thee gyve

Twenty marke to thy fee.'

151.

'I have a maister,' sayde Litell Johnn,

'A curteys knight is he;

May ye levë gete of hym,

The better may it be.'

152.

The sherif gate Litell John

Twelve monethës of the knight;

Therefore he gave him right anone

A gode hors and a wight.

153.

153.4 To give him his full reward.

Nowe is Litell John the sherifes man,

God lende us well to spede!

But alwey thought Lytell John

To quyte hym wele his mede.

154.

154.2 'leutye,' loyalty.

'Nowe so God me helpe,' sayde Litell John,

'And by my true leutye,

I shall be the worst servaunt to hym

That ever yet had he.'

155.

155.4 'foriete,' forgotten.

It fell upon a Wednesday

The sherif on huntynge was gone,

And Litel John lay in his bed,

And was foriete at home.

156.

Therfore he was fastinge

Til it was past the none;

'Gode sir stuarde, I pray to thee,

Gyve me my dynere,' saide Litell John.

157.

'It is longe for Grenëlefe

Fastinge thus for to be;

Therfor I pray thee, sir stuarde,

Mi dyner gif me.'

158.

'Shalt thou never ete ne drynke' saide the stuarde,

'Tyll my lorde be come to towne.'

'I make myn avowe to God,' saide Litell John,

'I had lever to crake thy crowne.'

159.

The boteler was full uncurteys,

There he stode on flore;

He start to the botery

And shet fast the dore.

160.

160.⁴ 'go' = walk.

Lytell Johnn gave the boteler suche a tap

His backe went nere in two;

Though he lived an hundred ier,

The wors shuld he go.

161.

161.³ 'lyveray,' purveyance.

He sporned the dore with his fote;

It went open wel and fyne;

And there he made large lyveray,

Bothe of ale and of wyne.

162.

'Sith ye wol nat dyne,' sayde Litell John,

'I shall gyve you to drinke;

And though ye lyve an hundred wynter,

On Lytel Johnn ye shall thinke.'

163.

Litell John ete, and Litel John drank,

The while that he wolde;

The sherife had in his kechyn a coke,

A stoute man and a bolde.

164.

'I make myn avowe to God,' said the coke,

'Thou arte a shrewde hynde

In ani hous for to dwel,

For to aske thus to dyne.'

165.

And there he lent Litell John

Godë strokis thre;

'I make myn avowe to God,' sayde Lytell John,

'These strokis lyked well me.

166.

'Thou arte a bolde man and hardy,

And so thinketh me;

And or I pas fro this place

Assayed better shalt thou be.'

167.

Lytell Johnn drew a ful gode sworde,

The coke took another in hande;

They thought no thynge for to fle,

But stifly for to stande.

168.

168.[2] 'Two mylë way' = the time it takes to go two miles. See *Early English Lyrics*, cxxvi. 55, and note.

168.⁴ 'mountnaunce,' duration.

There they faught sore togedere

Two mylë way and well more;

Myght nether other harme done,

The mountnaunce of an owre.

169.

'I make myn avowe to God,' sayde Litell Johnn,

'And by my true lewtë;

Thou art one of the best sworde-men

That ever yit sawe I me.

170.

'Cowdest thou shote as well in a bowe,

To grene wode thou shuldest with me,

And two times in the yere thy clothinge

Chaunged shuldë be;

171.

'And every yere of Robyn Hode

Twenty merke to thy fe.'

'Put up thy swerde,' saide the coke,

'And felowes woll we be.'

172.

172.² 'nowmbles,' entrails: cf. 32.⁴.

Thanne he fet to Lytell Johnn

The nowmbles of a do,

Gode brede, and full gode wyne;

They ete and drank theretoo.

173.

And when they had dronkyn well,

Theyre trouthes togeder they plight

That they wolde be with Robyn

That ylkë samë nyght.

174.

They dyd them to the tresoure-hows,

As fast as they myght gone;

The lokkes, that were of full gode stele,

They brake them everichone.

175.

175.³ 'Pecis,' cups; 'masars,' bowls.

They toke away the silver vessell,

And all that thei might get;

Pecis, masars, ne sponis,

Wolde thei not forget.

176.

Also they toke the godë pens,

Thre hundred pounde and more,

And did them streyte to Robyn Hode,

Under the grene wode hore.

177.

177.² Cf. *Child Waters*, 2.² (First Series, p. 37).

'God thee save, my dere mayster,

And Criste thee save and se!'

And thanne sayde Robyn to Litell Johnn,

'Welcome myght thou be.

178.

'Also be that fayre yeman

Thou bryngest there with thee;

What tydyngës fro Notyngham?

Lytill Johnn, tell thou me.'

179.

'Well thee gretith the proude sheryf,

And sendeth thee here by me

His coke and his silver vessell,

And thre hundred pounde and thre.'

180.

'I make myne avowe to God,' sayde Robyn,

'And to the Trenytë,

It was never by his gode wyll

This gode is come to me.'

181.

Lytyll Johnn there hym bethought

On a shrewde wyle;

Fyve myle in the forest he ran,

Hym happëd all his wyll.

182.

Than he met the proude sheref,

Huntynge with houndes and horne;

Lytell Johnn coude of curtesye,

And knelyd hym beforne.

183.

183.[2] See 177.[2] and note.

183.[3] 'shryef' may be a misprint, but 'shreeve' is another spelling of 'sheriff.'

'God thee save, my dere mayster,

Ande Criste thee save and se!'

'Reynolde Grenelefe,' sayde the shryef,

'Where hast thou nowe be?'

184.

'I have be in this forest;

- 55 -

A fayre syght can I se;

It was one of the fayrest syghtes

That ever yet sawe I me.

185.

185.⁴ 'bydene,' together.

'Yonder I sawe a ryght fayre harte,

His coloure is of grene;

Seven score of dere upon a herde

Be with hym all bydene.

186.

186.¹ 'tyndes' = tynes, forks of the antlers.

186.⁴ 'slo,' slay.

'Their tyndes are so sharp, maister,

Of sexty, and well mo,

That I durst not shote for drede,

Lest they wolde me slo.'

187.

'I make myn avowe to God,' sayde the shyref,

'That syght wolde I fayne se.'

'Buske you thyderwarde, my dere mayster,

Anone, and wende with me.'

188.

The sherif rode, and Litell Johnn

Of fote he was full smerte,

And whane they came before Robyn,

'Lo, sir, here is the mayster-herte.'

189.

Still stode the proude sherief,

A sory man was he;

'Wo the worthe, Raynolde Grenelefe,

Thou hast betrayed nowe me.'

190.

'I make myn avowe to God,' sayde Litell Johnn,

'Mayster, ye be to blame;

I was mysserved of my dynere

When I was with you at home.'

191.

Sone he was to souper sette,

And served well with silver white,

And when the sherif sawe his vessell,

For sorowe he myght nat ete.

192.

'Make glad chere,' sayde Robyn Hode,

'Sherif, for charitë,

And for the love of Litill Johnn

Thy lyfe I graunt to thee.'

193.

Whan they had soupëd well,

The day was al gone;

Robyn commaunded Litell Johnn

To drawe of his hosen and his shone;

194.

194.[3] 'toke,' gave.

His kirtell, and his cote of pie,

That was fured well and fine,

And toke hym a grene mantel,

To lap his body therein.

195.

Robyn commaundyd his wight yonge men,

Under the grene-wode tree,

They shulde lye in that same sute

That the sherif myght them see.

196.

All nyght lay the proude sherif

In his breche and in his schert;

No wonder it was, in grene wode,

Though his sydës gan to smerte.

197.

'Make glad chere,' sayde Robyn Hode,

'Sheref, for charitë;

For this is our ordre i-wys

Under the grene-wode tree.'

198.

198.[2] 'ankir,' anchorite, hermit.

'This is harder order,' sayde the sherief,

'Than any ankir or frere;

For all the golde in mery Englonde

I wolde nat longe dwell her.'

199.

'All this twelve monthes,' sayde Robin,

'Thou shalt dwell with me;

I shall thee techë, proude sherif,

An outlawe for to be.'

200.

200.[1] 'Or,' ere.

'Or I be here another nyght,' sayde the sherif,

'Robyn, nowe pray I thee,

Smyte of min hede rather to-morrowe,

And I forgyve it thee.

201.

'Lat me go,' than sayde the sherif,

'For sayntë charitë,

And I woll be the bestë frende

That ever yet had ye.'

202.

202.³ 'awayte me scathe,' lie in wait to do me harm.

'Thou shalt swere me an othe,' sayde Robyn,

'On my bright bronde;

Shalt thou never awayte me scathe

By water ne by lande.

203.

'And if thou fynde any of my men,

By nyght or by day,

Upon thyn othë thou shalt swere

To helpe them that thou may.'

204.

204.⁴ *i.e.* as ever a hip (berry of the wild rose) is of its stone.

Now hath the sherif sworne his othe,

And home he began to gone;

He was as full of grenë-wode

As ever was hepe of stone.

THE FOURTH FYTTE (205-280)

ARGUMENT.—Robin Hood will not dine until he has 'his pay,' and he therefore sends Little John with Much and Scarlok to wait for an 'unketh gest.' They capture a monk of St. Mary Abbey, and Robin Hood makes him disgorge eight hundred pounds. The monk, we are told, was on his way to London to take proceedings against the knight.

In due course the knight, who was left at the end of the second fytte at the wrestling-match, arrives to pay his debt to Robin Hood; who, however, refuses to receive it, saying that Our Lady had discharged the loan already.

The admirable, naïvely-told episode of Our Lady's method of repaying money lent on her security, is not without parallels, some of which Child points out (III. 53-4).

THE FOURTH FYTTE

    205.

    THE sherif dwelled in Notingham;

    He was fayne he was agone;

    And Robyn and his mery men

    Went to wode anone.

    206.

    'Go we to dyner,' sayde Littell Johnn;

    Robyn Hode sayde, 'Nay;

    For I drede Our Lady be wroth with me,

    For she sent me nat my pay.'

    207.

    'Have no doute, maister,' sayde Litell Johnn;

    'Yet is nat the sonne at rest;

    For I dare say, and savely swere.

    The knight is true and truste.'

    208.

    208., 209. A repetition of 17 and 18.

'Take thy bowe in thy hande,' sayde Robyn,

'Late Much wende with thee,

And so shal Wyllyam Scarlok,

And no man abyde with me.

209.

'And walke up under the Sayles,

And to Watlynge-strete,

And wayte after some unketh gest;

Up chaunce ye may them mete.

210.

'Whether he be messengere,

Or a man that myrthës can,

Of my good he shall have some,

Yf he be a porë man.'

211.

211.² 'tray and tene,' grief and vexation.

Forth then stert Lytel Johan,

Half in tray and tene,

And gyrde hym with a full good swerde,

Under a mantel of grene.

212.

They went up to the Sayles,

These yemen all thre;

They loked est, they loked west,

They myght no man se.

213.

213. *i.e.* Benedictines.

But as they loked in Bernysdale,

By the hyë waye,

Than were they ware of two blacke monkes,
Eche on a good palferay.

214.

214.³ 'wedde,' wager.

Then bespake Lytell Johan,
To Much he gan say,
'I dare lay my lyfe to wedde,
That these monkes have brought our pay.

215.

215.² 'frese' occurs nowhere else, and its meaning is unknown.

215.³ 'seker and sad,' resolute and staunch.

'Make glad chere,' sayd Lytell Johan,
'And frese your bowes of ewe,
And loke your hertes be seker and sad,
Your strynges trusty and trewe.

216.

216.² 'somers' = sumpters, pack-horses.

'The monke hath two and fifty men,
And seven somers full stronge;
There rydeth no bysshop in this londe
So ryally, I understond.

217.

'Brethern,' sayd Lytell Johan,
'Here are no more but we thre;
But we bryngë them to dyner,
Our mayster dare we not se.

218.

218.² 'prese,' crowd.

'Bende your bowes,' sayd Lytell Johan,

'Make all yon prese to stonde;
The formost monke, his lyfe and his deth
Is closëd in my honde.

219.

'Abyde, chorle monke,' sayd Lytell Johan,
'No ferther that thou gone;
Yf thou doost, by dere worthy God,
Thy deth is in my honde.

220.

'And evyll thryfte on thy hede,' sayd Lytell Johan,
'Ryght under thy hattë's bonde,
For thou hast made our mayster wroth,
He is fastynge so longe.'

221.

'Who is your mayster?' sayd the monke.
Lytell Johan sayd, 'Robyn Hode.'
'He is a stronge thefe,' sayd the monke,
'Of hym herd I never good.'

222.

'Thou lyest,' than sayd Lytell Johan,
'And that shall rewë thee;
He is a yeman of the forest,
To dyne he hath bodë thee.'

223.

Much was redy with a bolte,
Redly and anone,
He set the monke to-fore the brest,
To the grounde that he can gone.

224.

Of two and fyfty wyght yonge yemen,

There abode not one,

Saf a lytell page and a grome,

To lede the somers with Lytel Johan.

225.

225.² 'lefe,' pleased, willing.

225.⁴ 'Maugre,' in spite of.

They brought the monke to the lodgë-dore,

Whether he were loth or lefe,

For to speke with Robyn Hode,

Maugre in theyr tethe.

226.

Robyn dyde adowne his hode,

The monke whan that he se;

The monke was not so curteyse,

His hode then let he be.

227.

227.³ 'no force,' no matter.

'He is a chorle, mayster, by dere worthy God,'

Than sayd Lytell Johan.

'Thereof no force,' sayd Robyn,

'For curteysy can he none.

228.

'How many men,' sayd Robyn,

'Had this monke, Johan?'

'Fyfty and two whan that we met,

But many of them be gone.'

229.

229.² 'felaushyp' = our fellows.

'Let blowe a horne,' sayd Robyn,

'That felaushyp may us knowe.'

Seven score of wyght yemen,

Came pryckynge on a rowe.

230.

230.² 'raye,' striped cloth.

And everych of them a good mantell

Of scarlet and of raye;

All they came to good Robyn,

To wyte what he wolde say.

231.

They made the monke to wasshe and wype,

And syt at his denere.

Robyn Hode and Lytell Johan

They served him both in fere.

232.

232.⁴ 'avowë,' patron.

'Do gladly, monke,' sayd Robyn.

'Gramercy, syr,' sayd he.

'Where is your abbay, whan ye are at home,

And who is your avowë?'

233.

'Saynt Mary abbay,' sayd the monke,

'Though I be symple here.'

'In what offyce?' said Robyn:

'Syr, the hye selerer.'

234.

234.² A common form of asseveration = 'upon my life'; 'the' = thrive. Cf. 243.⁴.

'Ye be the more welcome,' sayd Robyn,

'So ever mote I the!

Fyll of the best wyne,' sayd Robyn,

'This monke shall drynke to me.

235.

'But I have grete mervayle,' sayd Robyn,

'Of all this longë day;

I drede Our Lady be wroth with me,

She sent me not my pay.'

236.

'Have no doute, mayster,' sayd Lytell Johan,

'Ye have no nede, I saye;

This monke hath brought it, I dare well swere,

For he is of her abbay.'

237.

237.[1] 'borowe,' security.

'And she was a borowe,' sayd Robyn,

'Betwene a knyght and me,

Of a lytell money that I hym lent,

Under the grene-wode tree.

238.

'And yf thou hast that sylver ibrought,

I pray thee let me se;

And I shall helpë thee eftsones,

Yf thou have nede to me.'

239.

239.[2] 'chere,' countenance.

The monke swore a full grete othe,

With a sory chere,

'Of the borowehode thou spekest to me,

Herde I never ere.'

240.

'I make myn avowe to God,' sayd Robyn,

'Monke, thou art to blame;

For God is holde a ryghtwys man,

And so is his dame.

241.

'Thou toldest with thyn ownë tonge,

Thou may not say nay,

How thou arte her servaunt,

And servest her every day.

242.

'And thou art made her messengere,

My money for to pay;

Therefore I cun the morë thanke

Thou arte come at thy day.

243.

243.[4] See 234.[2] and note.

'What is in your cofers?' sayd Robyn,

'Trewe than tell thou me.'

'Syr,' he sayd, 'twenty marke,

Al so mote I the.'

244.

244.[3] 'myster,' need.

'Yf there be no more,' sayd Robyn,

'I wyll not one peny;

Yf thou hast myster of ony more,

Syr, more I shall lende to thee.

245.

'And yf I fyndë more,' sayd Robyn,

'I-wys thou shalte it forgone;

For of thy spendynge-sylver, monke,

Thereof wyll I ryght none.

246.

'Go nowe forthe, Lytell Johan,

And the trouth tell thou me;

If there be no more but twenty marke,

No peny that I se.'

247.

247.[3] 'male,' trunk. See 134.[2] and 374.[1].

Lytell Johan spred his mantell downe,

As he had done before,

And he tolde out of the monkës male

Eyght hondred pounde and more.

248.

Lytell Johan let it lye full styll,

And went to his mayster in hast;

'Syr,' he sayd, 'the monke is trewe ynowe,

Our Lady hath doubled your cast.'

249.

'I make myn avowe to God,' sayd Robyn—

'Monke, what tolde I thee?—

Our Lady is the trewest woman

That ever yet founde I me.

250.

250.[3] 'pay,' liking.

'By dere worthy God,' sayd Robyn,

'To seche all Englond thorowe,

Yet founde I never to my pay

A moche better borowe.

251.

251.2 'hende,' gracious.

'Fyll of the best wyne, and do hym drynke,' sayd Robyn,

'And grete well thy lady hende,

And yf she have nede to Robyn Hode,

A frende she shall hym fynde.

252.

'And yf she nedeth ony more sylver,

Come thou agayne to me,

And, by this token she hath me sent,

She shall have such thre.'

253.

253.2 'mote,' meeting.

The monke was goynge to London ward,

There to hold grete mote,

The knyght that rode so hye on hors,

To brynge hym under fote.

254.

254.3 'reves,' bailiffs.

'Whether be ye away?' sayd Robyn.

'Syr, to maners in this londe,

To reken with our reves,

That have done moch wronge.'

255.

'Come now forth, Lytell Johan,

And harken to my tale;

A better yemen I knowe none,

To seke a monkës male.'

256.

256.¹ 'corser,' coffer (?).

'How moch is in yonder other corser?' sayd Robyn,

'The soth must we see.'

'By Our Lady,' than sayd the monke,

'That were no curteysye,

257.

'To bydde a man to dyner,

And syth hym bete and bynde.'

'It is our olde maner,' sayd Robyn,

'To leve but lytell behynde.'

258.

The monke toke the hors with spore,

No lenger wolde he abyde:

'Askë to drynke,' than sayd Robyn,

'Or that ye forther ryde.'

259.

'Nay, for God,' than sayd the monke,

'Me reweth I cam so nere;

For better chepe I myght have dyned

In Blythe or in Dankestere.'

260.

'Grete well your abbot,' sayd Robyn,

'And your pryour, I you pray,

And byd hym send me such a monke

To dyner every day.'

261.

Now lete we that monke be styll,

And speke we of that knyght:

Yet he came to holde his day,

Whyle that it was lyght.

262.

He dyde him streyt to Bernysdale,

Under the grene-wode tre,

And he founde there Robyn Hode,

And all his mery meynë.

263.

The knyght lyght doune of his good palfray,

Robyn whan he gan see;

So curteysly he dyde adoune his hode,

And set hym on his knee.

264.

'God the savë, Robyn Hode,

And all this company!'

'Welcome be thou, gentyll knyght,

And ryght welcome to me.'

265.

Than bespake hym Robyn Hode,

To that knyght so fre;

'What nede dryveth thee to grene-wode?

I praye thee, syr knyght, tell me.

266.

'And welcome be thou, gentyll knyght,

Why hast thou be so longe?'

'For the abbot and the hye justyce

Wolde have had my londe.'

267.

'Hast thou thy londe agayne?' sayd Robyn;

'Treuth than tell thou me.'

'Ye, for God,' sayd the knyght,

'And that thanke I God and thee.

268.

'But take no grefe, that I have be so longe;

I came by a wrastelynge,

And there I holpe a pore yeman,

With wronge was put behynde.'

269.

'Nay, for God,' sayd Robyn,

'Syr knyght, that thanke I thee;

What man that helpeth a good yeman,

His frende than wyll I be.'

270.

'Have here foure hondred pounde,' than sayd the knyght,

'The whiche ye lent to me;

And here is also twenty marke

For your curteysy.'

271.

271.[2] 'broke,' enjoy. Cf. 274.[3] and 279.[3].

'Nay, for God,' than sayd Robyn,

'Thou broke it well for ay;

For Our Lady, by her hye selerer,

Hath sent to me my pay.

272.

'And yf I toke it i-twyse,

A shame it were to me;

But trewely, gentyll knyght,

Welcome arte thou to me.'

273.

273.² 'leugh,' laughed.

Whan Robyn had tolde his tale,

He leugh and had good chere:

'By my trouthe,' then sayd the knyght,

'Your money is redy here.'

274.

'Broke it well,' said Robyn,

'Thou gentyll knyght so fre;

And welcome be thou, gentyll knyght,

Under my trystell-tre.

275.

275.² 'ifedred,' feathered.

'But what shall these bowës do?' sayd Robyn,

'And these arowes ifedred fre?'

'By God,' than sayd the knyght,

'A pore present to thee.'

276.

'Come now forth, Lytell Johan,

And go to my treasurë,

And brynge me there foure hondred pounde,

The monke over-tolde it me.

277.

'Have here foure hondred pounde,

Thou gentyll knyght and trewe,

And bye hors and havnes good,

And gylte thy spores all newe.

278.

'And yf thou fayle ony spendynge,

Com to Robyn Hode,

And by my trouth thou shalt none fayle,

The whyles I have any good.

279.

'And broke well thy foure hondred pound,

Whiche I lent to the,

And make thy selfe no more so bare,

By the counsell of me.'

280.

Thus than holpe hym good Robyn,

The knyght all of his care:

God, that syt in heven hye,

Graunte us well to fare!

THE FIFTH FYTTE (281-316)

ARGUMENT.—The story now returns to the Sheriff of Nottingham, and relates how he offered a prize for the best archer in the north. Robin Hood, hearing of this match, determines to go to it, and to test the sheriff's faith to his oath (see the Third Fytte, stt. 202-4). Robin wins the prize, and is starting home to the greenwood, when the sheriff recognises and attacks him, but is beaten off by a shower of arrows. Robin and his men retire, shooting as they go, until they come to a castle. Here dwells the knight to whom Robin had lent the money—'Sir Richard at the Lee.' He takes in Robin and his men, and defies the sheriff; Robin, he says, shall spend forty days with him.

This fytte is no doubt based on some single lost ballad of a shooting-match at which Robin was victorious, and at which the Sheriff of Nottingham attempted in vain to arrest him. But the compiler of the *Gest* has carefully linked it to the preceding fyttes by such references as Robin's determination to try the sheriff's faith (st. 287), which is made clear in stt. 296-8; and the identification of the knight whose castle protects Robin and his men with the knight to whom the money had been lent (stt. 310-312).

THE FIFTH FYTTE

    281.

    NOW hath the knyght his leve i-take,

    And wente hym on his way;

    Robyn Hode and his mery men

    Dwelled styll full many a day.

    282.

    282.[4] 'dyde' = caused to: cf. 'do you to wit.' —GUMMERE.

    Lyth and listen, gentil men,

    And herken what I shall say,

    How the proud sheryfe of Notyngham

    Dyde crye a full fayre play;

    283.

    283.[3] 'allther best,' best of all: cp. 9.[4].

That all the best archers of the north

Sholde come upon a day,

And he that shoteth allther best

The game shall bere away.

284.

284.³ 'fynly,' goodly.

He that shoteth allther best,

Furthest fayre and lowe,

At a payre of fynly buttes,

Under the grene wode shawe,

285.

A ryght good arowe he shall have,

The shaft of sylver whyte,

The hede and feders of ryche rede golde,

In Englond is none lyke.

286.

This than herde good Robyn

Under his trystell-tre:

'Make you redy, ye wyght yonge men;

That shotynge wyll I se.

287.

287.³ 'wete,' know.

287.⁴ 'and yf' =
Remainder of note invisible in the original; may be "and yf = if".

'Buske you, my mery yonge men;

Ye shall go with me;

And I wyll wete the shryvës fayth,

Trewe and yf he be.'

288.

288.² 'fedred fre,' fully feathered.

Whan they had theyr bowes i-bent,
Theyr takles fedred fre,
Seven score of wyght yonge men
Stode by Robyn's kne.

289.

Whan they cam to Notyngham,
The buttes were fayre and longe;
Many was the bolde archere
That shoted with bowës stronge.

290.

290.² 'hevede' = head, *i.e.* life.

'There shall but syx shote with me;
The other shal kepe my hevede,
And standë with good bowës bent,
That I be not desceyved.'

291.

The fourth outlawe his bowe gan bende,
And that was Robyn Hode,
And that behelde the proud sheryfe,
All by the but as he stode.

292.

292.² 'slist,' sliced, split.

Thryës Robyn shot about,
And alway he slist the wand,
And so dyde good Gylberte
With the whytë hande.

293.

Lytell Johan and good Scatheloke

Were archers good and fre;

Lytell Much and good Reynolde,

The worste wolde they not be.

294.

Whan they had shot aboute,

These archours fayre and good,

Evermore was the best,

For soth, Robyn Hode.

295.

295.³ 'yeft,' gift, prize.

Hym was delyvred the good arowe,

For best worthy was he;

He toke the yeft so curteysly;

To grenë-wode wolde he.

296.

They cryed out on Robyn Hode,

And grete hornës gan they blowe:

'Wo worth the, treason!' sayd Robyn,

'Full evyl thou art to knowe.

297.

297.³ 'behotë,' didst promise.

'And wo be thou, thou proudë sheryf,

Thus gladdynge thy gest!

Other wyse thou behotë me

In yonder wylde forest.

298.

298.³ 'wedde,' forfeit.

298.⁴ 'lewtë,' loyalty, faith.

'But had I thee in grenë-wode,

Under my trystell-tre,

Thou sholdest leve me a better wedde

Than thy trewe lewtë.'

299.

Full many a bowë there was bent,

And arowës let they glyde;

Many a kyrtell there was rent,

And hurt many a syde.

300.

300.[4] 'blyve,' quickly.

The outlawes shot was so stronge

That no man might them dryve,

And the proud sheryfës men,

They fled away full blyve.

301.

301.[1] 'busshement,' ambuscade: 'to-broke,' broken up.

Robyn sawe the busshement to-broke,

In grene wode he wolde have be;

Many an arowe there was shot

Amonge that company.

302.

Lytell Johan was hurte full sore,

With an arowe in his kne,

That he myght neyther go nor ryde;

It was full grete pytë.

303.

'Mayster,' then sayd Lytell Johan,

'If ever thou lovedst me,

And for that ylkë lordës love

That dyed upon a tre,

304.

304.[1] 'medes,' wages.

'And for the medes of my servyce,

That I have servëd thee,

Lete never the proudë sheryf

Alyve now fyndë me.

305.

'But take out thy brownë swerde,

And smyte all of my hede,

And gyve me woundës depe and wyde;

No lyfe on me be lefte.'

306.

'I wolde not that,' sayd Robyn,

'Johan, that thou were slawe,

For all the golde in mery Englonde,

Though it lay now on a rawe.'

307.

'God forbede,' sayd Lytell Much,

'That dyed on a tre,

That thou sholdest, Lytell Johan,

Parte our company.'

308.

Up he toke hym on his backe,

And bare hym well a myle;

Many a tyme he layd him downe,

And shot another whyle.

309.

Then was there a fayre castell,

A lytell within the wode;

Double-dyched it was about,

And walled, by the rode.

310.

And there dwelled that gentyll knyght,

Syr Rychard at the Lee,

That Robyn had lent his good,

Under the grene-wode tree.

311.

In he toke good Robyn,

And all his company:

'Welcome be thou, Robyn Hode,

Welcome arte thou to me;

312.

'And moche I thanke thee of thy comfort,

And of thy curteysye,

And of thy gretë kyndënesse,

Under the grene-wode tre.

306.[4] 'on a rawe,' in a row; cf. 60.[2].

313.

'I love no man in all this worlde

So much as I do thee;

For all the proud sheryf of Notyngham,

Ryght here shalt thou be.

314.

'Shyt the gates, and drawe the brydge,

And let no man come in,

And arme you well, and make you redy,

And to the walles ye wynne.

315.

315.¹ 'behote,' promise; cf. 297.³.

315.³ 'wonnest,' dwellest.

'For one thynge, Robyn, I the behote;

I swere by Saynt Quyntyne,

These forty dayes thou wonnest with me,

To soupe, ete, and dyne.'

316.

Bordes were layde, and clothes were spredde,

Redely and anone;

Robyn Hode and his mery men

To mete can they gone.

THE SIXTH FYTTE (317-353)

ARGUMENT.—The Sheriff of Nottingham secures the assistance of the High Sheriff, and besets the knight's castle, accusing him of harbouring the king's enemies. The knight bids him appeal to the king, saying he will 'avow' (*i.e.* make good or justify) all he has done, on the pledge of all his lands. The sheriffs raise the siege and go to London, where the king says he will be at Nottingham in two weeks and will capture both the knight and Robin Hood. The sheriff returns home to get together a band of archers to assist the king; but meanwhile Robin has escaped to the greenwood. However, the sheriff lies in wait for the knight, captures him and takes him bound to Nottingham. The knight's lady rides to Robin and begs him to save her lord; whereupon Robin and his men hasten to Nottingham, kill the sheriff, release the knight, and carry him off to the greenwood.

The latter episode—of Robin's release, at the request of his wife, of a knight taken captive by the sheriff—comes probably from a separate ballad: *Robin Hood rescuing Three Squires* tells a similar story. This the compiler of the *Gest* has apparently woven in with the story of the previous fyttes, though he has not done so very thoroughly (*e.g.*, the inconsistency of Robin's question to the knight's wife, 'What man hath your lord i-take?' with his knowledge of the knight's defiance of the sheriff). The compiler has also neatly prepared the way for the introduction of the seventh and eighth fyttes by the knight's appeal to the king; but, having done so, he has apparently forgotten the king's undertaking to come to Nottingham, and has allowed the sheriff to anticipate that plan and capture the knight without assistance.

THE SIXTH FYTTE

 317.

 LYTHE and lysten, gentylmen,

 And herkyn to your songe;

 Howe the proudë shyref of Notyngham,

 And men of armys stronge,

 318.

 Full fast cam to the hyë shyref,

 The contrë up to route,

 And they besette the knyghtës castell,

The wallës all aboute.

319.

The proudë shyref loude gan crye,

And sayde, 'Thou traytour knight,

Thou kepest here the kynges enemys,

Agaynst the lawe and right.'

320.

320.[2] 'dyght,' concerted.

'Syr, I wyll avowe that I have done,

The dedys that here be dyght,

Upon all the landës that I have,

As I am a trewë knyght.

321.

'Wende furth, sirs, on your way,

And do no more to me

Tyll ye wyt oure kyngës wille,

What he wyll say to thee.'

322.

322.[3] 'yede,' went.

The shyref thus had his answere,

Without any lesynge;

Forth he yede to London towne,

All for to tel our kinge.

323.

Ther he telde him of that knight,

And eke of Robyn Hode,

And also of the bolde archars,

That were soo noble and gode.

324.

- 84 -

'He wyll avowe that he hath done,

To mayntene the outlawes stronge;

He wyll be lorde, and set you at nought,

In all the northe londe.'

325.

'I wil be at Notyngham,' sayde our kynge,

'Within this fourteennyght,

And take I wyll Robyn Hode

And so I wyll that knight.

326.

326.[3] 'ordeyn,' levy, summon.

'Go nowe home, shyref,' sayde our kynge,

'And do as I byd thee;

And ordeyn gode archers ynowe,

Of all the wyde contrë.'

327.

The shyref had his leve i-take,

And went hym on his way;

And Robyn Hode to grenë wode,

Upon a certen day.

328.

328. See st. 302.

And Lytel John was hole of the arowe

That shot was in his kne,

And dyd hym streyght to Robyn Hode,

Under the grene wode tree.

329.

329.[4] 'tene,' anger. 'Thereof' means 'of Robin's escape.'

Robyn Hode walked in the forest,

Under the levys grene;

The proud shyref of Notyngham

Thereof he had grete tene.

330.

The shyref there fayled of Robyn Hode,

He myght not have his pray;

Than he awayted this gentyll knyght,

Bothe by nyght and day.

331.

Ever he wayted the gentyll knyght,

Syr Richarde at the Lee,

As he went on haukynge by the ryver-syde

And lete his haukës flee.

332.

Toke he there this gentyll knight,

With men of armys stronge,

And led hym to Notynghamwarde,

Bounde bothe fote and hande.

333.

333.[3] 'lever,' rather.

The sheref sware a full grete othe,

Bi him that dyed on rode,

He had lever than an hundred pound

That he had Robyn Hode.

334.

This harde the knyghtës wyfe,

A fayr lady and a free;

She set hir on a gode palfrey,
To grene wode anone rode she.
335.
Whanne she cam in the forest,
Under the grene wode tree,
Fonde she there Robyn Hode,
And all his fayre menë.
336.

336.4 'bone,' boon.

'God thee savë, gode Robyn,
And all thy company;
For Our derë Ladyes sake,
A bonë graunte thou me.
337.
'Late never my wedded lorde
Shamefully slayne be;
He is fast bowne to Notinghamwarde,
For the love of thee.'
338.

338.4, 339.1: supplied from later versions.

Anone than saide goode Robyn
To that lady so fre,
'What man hath your lorde ytake?'
['The proude shirife,' than sayd she.
339.
'You may them overtake, Robyn,]
For soth as I thee say;
He is nat yet thre mylës
Passed on his way.'

334.[1] 'harde,' = heard.

340.

340.[2] 'wode,' mad.

Up than sterte gode Robyn,

As man that had ben wode:

'Buske you, my mery men,

For hym that dyed on rode.

341.

'And he that this sorowe forsaketh,

By hym that dyed on tre,

Shall he never in grenë wode

No lenger dwel with me.'

342.

Sone there were gode bowës bent,

Mo than seven score;

Hedge ne dyche spared they none

That was them before.

343.

'I make myn avowe to God,' sayde Robyn,

'The sherif wolde I fayne see;

And if I may him take,

I-quyt then shall he be.'

344.

And when they came to Notingham,

They walked in the strete;

And with the proudë sherif i-wys

Sonë can they mete.

345.

'Abyde, thou proudë sherif,' he sayde,

'Abyde, and speke with me;

Of some tidinges of oure kinge

I wolde fayne here of thee.

346.

346.² 'this' = thus.

'This seven yere, by dere worthy God,

Ne yede I this fast on fote;

I make myn avowe to God, thou proudë sherif,

It is not for thy gode.'

347.

Robyn bent a full goode bowe,

An arrowe he drowe at wyll;

He hit so the proudë sherife

Upon the grounde he lay full still.

348.

348.¹ 'And or' = ere.

And or he myght up aryse,

On his fete to stonde,

He smote of the sherifs hede

With his brightë bronde.

349.

349.² 'cheve,' gain, win.

'Lye thou there, thou proudë sherife;

Evyll mote thou cheve!

There myght no man to thee truste

The whyles thou were a lyve.'

350.

350.[4] 'bydene,' one after another.

His men drewe out theyr bryght swerdes,

That were so sharpe and kene,

And layde on the sheryves men,

And dryved them downe bydene.

351.

351.[3] 'toke,' gave.

Robyn stert to that knyght,

And cut a two his bonde,

And toke hym in his hand a bowe,

And bad hym by hym stonde.

352.

'Leve thy hors thee behynde,

And lerne for to renne;

Thou shalt with me to grenë wode,

Through myrë, mosse, and fenne.

353.

'Thou shalt with me to grenë wode,

Without ony leasynge,

Tyll that I have gete us grace

Of Edwarde, our comly kynge.'

THE SEVENTH FYTTE (354-417)

ARGUMENT.—The king, coming with a great array to Nottingham to take Robin Hood and the knight, and finding nothing but a great scarcity of deer, is wondrous wroth, and promises the knight's lands to any one who will bring him his head. For half a year the king has no news of Robin; at length, at the suggestion of a forester, he disguises himself as an abbot and five of his men as monks, and goes into the greenwood. He is met and stopped by Robin Hood, gives up forty pounds to him, and alleges he is a messenger from the king. Thereupon Robin entertains him and his men on the king's own deer, and the outlaws hold an archery competition, Robin smiting those that miss. At his last shot, Robin himself misses, and asks the abbot to smite him in his turn. The abbot gives him such a buffet that Robin is nearly felled; on looking more closely, he recognises the king, of whom he and his men ask pardon on their knees. The king grants it, on condition that they will enter his service. Robin agrees, but reserves the right to return to the greenwood if he mislikes the court.

This fytte is based on the story, extremely common and essentially popular, especially in England, of a meeting between a king in disguise and one of his subjects. Doubtless there was a ballad of Robin Hood and the king; but the only one we possess, *The King's Disguise and Friendship with Robin Hood*, is a late and a loose paraphrase of this fytte and the next. The commonest stories and ballads of this type in English are *The King and the Barker* (*i.e.* Tanner), *King Edward the Fourth and the Tanner of Tamworth*, *King James and the Tinker*, and *King Henry II. and the Miller of Mansfield*. Usually the point of the story is the lack of ceremony displayed by the subject, and the royal good-humour and largesse of the king.

There is only an arbitrary division between Fyttes VII. and VIII.; and one or two other points will be discussed in introducing the next and last fytte.

THE SEVENTH FYTTE

    354.

    354.[4] 'and yf' = if.

    THE kynge came to Notynghame,

    With knyghtës in grete araye,

    For to take that gentyll knyght

    And Robyn Hode, and yf he may.

355.

He askëd men of that countrë

After Robyn Hode,

And after that gentyll knyght,

That was so bolde and stout.

356.

Whan they had tolde hym the case

Our kynge understode ther tale,

And seased in his honde

The knyghtës londës all.

357.

357.³ Plumpton Park is said by Camden in his Britannia to be in Cumberland, east of Inglewood.

All the passe of Lancasshyre

He went both ferre and nere,

Tyll he came to Plomton Parke;

He faylyd many of his dere.

358.

358.³ 'unneth,' scarcely.

There our kynge was wont to se

Herdës many one,

He coud unneth fynde one dere,

That bare ony good home.

359.

The kynge was wonder wroth withall,

And swore by the Trynytë,

'I wolde I had Robyn Hode,

With eyen I myght hym se.

360.

'And he that wolde smyte of the knyghtës hede,

And brynge it to me,

He shall have the knyghtës londes,

Syr Rycharde at the Le.

361.

'I gyve it hym with my charter,

And sele it with my honde,

To have and holde for ever more,

In all mery Englonde.'

362.

Than bespake a fayre olde knyght,

That was treue in his fay:

'A, my leegë lorde the kynge,

One worde I shall you say.

363.

'There is no man in this countrë

May have the knyghtës londes,

Whyle Robyn Hode may ryde or gone,

And bere a bowe in his hondes,

364.

364.[2] 'The ball in the hood' is a very early colloquialism for the head.

'That he ne shall lese his hede,

That is the best ball in his hode:

Give it no man, my lorde the kynge,

That ye wyll any good.'

365.

Half a yere dwelled our comly kynge

In Notyngham, and well more;

Coude he not here of Robyn Hode,

In what countrë that he were.

366.

366.² 'halke,' hiding-place.

366.⁴ 'welt,' disposed of.

But alway went good Robyn

By halke and eke by hyll,

And alway slewe the kyngës dere,

And welt them at his wyll.

367.

367.¹ 'fostere,' forester.

Than bespake a proude fostere,

That stode by our kyngës kne:

'Yf ye wyll see good Robyn,

Ye must do after me.

368.

'Take fyve of the best knyghtes

That be in your lede,

And walke downe by yon abbay,

And gete you monkës wede.

369.

'And I wyll be your ledes-man,

And lede you the way,

And or ye come to Notyngham,

Myn hede then dare I lay,

370.

'That ye shall mete with good Robyn,

On lyve yf that he be;

Or ye come to Notyngham,

With eyen ye shall hym se.'

371.

371.¹ 'dyght,' dressed.

Full hastely our kynge was dyght,

were his knyghtës fyve,

Everych of them in monkës wede,

And hasted them thyder blyve.

372.

372.¹ 'cote' = cowl; here, however, not the hood, but the frock of a monk.

Our kynge was grete above his cole,

A brode hat on his crowne,

Ryght as he were abbot-lyke,

They rode up into the towne.

373.

373.⁴ 'covent' = convent (as in 'Covent Garden'), company of monks.

Styf botës our kynge had on,

Forsoth as I you say;

He rode syngynge to grenë wode;

The covent was clothed in graye.

374.

374.¹ 'male-hors,' pack-horse; 'somers,' sumpter-horses.

374.⁴ 'lynde,' trees.

His male-hors and his grete somers

Folowed our kynge behynde,

Tyll they came to grene wode,

A myle under the lynde.

375.

There they met with good Robyn,

Stondynge on the waye,

And so dyde many a bolde archere,

For soth as I you say.

376.

Robyn toke the kyngës hors,

Hastely in that stede,

And sayd, 'Syr abbot, by your leve,

A whyle ye must abyde.

377.

'We be yemen of this foreste,

Under the grene-wode tre;

We lyve by our kyngës dere,

Other shyft have not we.

378.

'And ye have chyrches and rentës both,

And gold full grete plentë;

Gyve us some of your spendynge,

For saynt charytë.'

379.

Than bespake our cumly kynge,

Anone than sayd he;

'I brought no more to grene-wode

But forty pounde with me.

380.

'I have layne at Notyngham,

This fourtynyght with our kynge,

And spent I have full moche good

On many a grete lordynge.

381.

'And I have but forty pounde,

No more than have I me:

But if I had an hondred pounde,

I wolde vouch it safe on thee.'

382.

382.³ 'Halfendell' = halfen deal (which survives in Somerset dialect), the half portion: *deal*, as in 'a great deal' = dole, or that which is dealt.

Robyn toke the forty pounde,

And departed it in two partye;

Halfendell he gave his mery men,

And bad them mery to be.

383.

Full curteysly Robyn gan say;

'Syr, have this for your spendyng;

We shall mete another day';

'Gramercy,' than sayd our kynge.

384.

'But well thee greteth Edwarde our kynge,

And sent to thee his seale,

And byddeth thee com to Notyngham,

Both to mete and mele.'

385.

385.¹ 'brode targe,' broad charter. Cf. a 'braid letter.'

He toke out the brode targe,

And sone he lete hym se;

Robyn coud his courteysy,

And set hym on his kne.

386.

'I love no man in all the worlde

So well as I do my kynge;

Welcome is my lordës seale;

And, monke, for thy tydynge,

387.

'Syr abbot, for thy tydynges,

To day thou shalt dyne with me,

For the love of my kynge,

Under my trystell-tre.'

388.

388.[4] 'dyghtande' (intended for a past participle), made ready.

Forth he lad our comly kynge,

Full fayre by the honde;

Many a dere there was slayne,

And full fast dyghtande.

389.

389.[4] 'on a row': cf. 306.[4].

Robyn toke a full grete home,

And loude he gan blowe;

Seven score of wyght yonge men

Came redy on a rowe.

390.

All they kneled on theyr kne,

Full fayre before Robyn:

The kynge sayd hymselfe untyll,

And swore by Saynt Austyn,

391.

391.² 'pyne,' passion.

'Here is a wonder semely sight;

Me thynketh, by Goddës pyne,

His men are more at his byddynge

Then my men be at myn.'

392.

Full hastely was theyr dyner i-dyght,

And therto gan they gone;

They served our kynge with all theyr myght,

Both Robyn and Lytell Johan.

393.

Anone before our kynge was set

The fattë venyson,

The good whyte brede, the good rede wyne,

And therto the fyne ale and browne.

394.

394.³ 'ylke,' same.

'Make good chere,' said Robyn,

'Abbot, for charytë;

And for this ylkë tydynge,

Blyssed mote thou be.

395.

395.² 'Or' = ere.

395.⁴ 'lende,' dwell.

'Now shalte thou se what lyfe we lede,

Or thou hens wende;

Than thou may enfourme our kynge,

Whan ye togyder lende.'

396.

Up they stertë all in hast,

Theyr bowes were smartly bent;

Our kynge was never so sore agast,

He wende to have be shente.

397.

397.[4] *i.e.* 'merkes,' distances between the 'yerdes' or rods.

Two yerdes there were up set,

Thereto gan they gange;

By fyfty pase, our kynge sayd,

The merkës were to longe.

398.

398.[4] *i.e.* his arrow he shall lose.

On every syde a rose-garlonde,

They shot under the lyne:

'Who so fayleth of the rose-garlonde,' sayd Robyn,

'His takyll he shall tyne,

399.

'And yelde it to his mayster,

Be it never so fyne;

For no man wyll I spare,

So drynke I ale or wyne;

400.

'And bere a buffet on his hede,

I-wys ryght all bare':

And all that fell in Robyns lote,

He smote them wonder sare.

401.

Twyse Robyn shot aboute,

And ever he cleved the wande,

And so dyde good Gylberte

With the Whytë Hande.

402.

Lytell Johan and good Scathelocke,

For nothynge wolde they spare;

When they fayled of the garlonde,

Robyn smote them full sore.

403.

At the last shot that Robyn shot,

For all his frendës fare,

Yet he fayled of the garlonde

Thre fyngers and mare.

404.

Than bespake good Gylberte,

And thus he gan say;

'Mayster,' he sayd, 'your takyll is lost;

Stande forth and take your pay.'

405.

'If it be so,' sayd Robyn,

'That may no better be,

Syr abbot, I delyver thee myn arowe,

I pray thee, syr, serve thou me.'

406.

'It falleth not for myn ordre,' sayd our kynge,

'Robyn, by thy leve,

For to smyte no good yeman,

For doute I sholde hym greve.'

407.

'Smyte on boldely,' sayd Robyn,

'I give thee largë leve':

Anone our kynge, with that worde,

He folde up his sleve,

408.

408.² 'yede,' went.

And sych a buffet he gave Robyn,

To grounde he yede full nere:

'I make myn avowe to God,' sayd Robyn,

'Thou arte a stalworthe frere.

409.

'There is pith in thyn arme,' sayd Robyn,

'I trowe thou canst well shete.'

Thus our kynge and Robyn Hode

Togeder gan they mete.

410.

410.² 'Wystly,' observantly, closely.

Robyn behelde our comly kynge

Wystly in the face,

So dyde Syr Rycharde at the Le,

And kneled downe in that place.

411.

And so dyde all the wylde outlawes,

Whan they se them knele:

'My lorde the kynge of Englonde,

Now I knowe you well.'

412.

'Mercy then, Robyn,' sayd our kynge,

'Under your trystyll-tre,

Of thy goodnesse and thy grace,

For my men and me!'

413.

'Yes, for God,' sayd Robyn,

'And also God me save,

I aske mercy, my lorde the kynge,

And for my men I crave.'

414.

414.² 'sent' = assent.

414.³ 'With that,' provided that, on condition that.

'Yes, for God,' than sayd our kynge,

'And therto sent I me,

With that thou leve the grenë-wode

And all thy company;

415.

'And come home, syr, to my courte,

And there dwell with me.'

'I make myn avowe to God,' sayd Robyn,

'And ryght so shall it be.

416.

'I wyll come to your courte,

Your servyse for to se,

And brynge with me of my men

Seven score and thre.

417.

417.[1] 'But,' unless.

417.[3] 'donne,' dun.

'But me lyke well your servyse,
I wyll come agayne full soone,
And shote at the donnë dere,
As I am wonte to done.'

THE EIGHTH FYTTE (418-456)

ARGUMENT.—For a jest, the king disguises himself and his men once more, this time in Lincoln green, which he purchases off Robin Hood. The whole party proceeds to Nottingham, where the appearance of so many green mantles causes a general flight of the inhabitants. The king, however, reveals himself, and after a feast, pardons the knight.

Robin dwells in the king's court for fifteen months, at the end of which time he has spent much money, and has lost all his men except Little John and Scathlock. He therefore begs the king's leave to go on a pilgrimage to a shrine of St. Mary Magdalen in Barnsdale, and the king consents, but allows him only seven nights' absence. Robin comes to the greenwood, and shoots a great hart; and on blowing his horn, seven score yeomen come and welcome him back, and he dwells two-and-twenty years in the greenwood. In the end he was betrayed by his kinswoman, the Prioress of Kirkesly Abbey, and her lover, Sir Roger of Doncaster.

It has been suggested (by Professor Brandl) that the episode of the king's disguise in green is an intentional variation of the episode in the Third Fytte, where the Sheriff of Nottingham is forced to wrap himself in a green mantle. In any case it is probable that most of this Eighth Fytte is the work of the compiler of the *Gest*; possibly even the delightful verses (stt. 445-6) in which the joy of greenwood life overcomes Robin.

One could wish the *Gest* ended with st. 450; but it is clear that the compiler knew of a ballad which narrated the death of Robin Hood, no doubt an earlier version of the *Robin Hood's Death* of the Percy Folio, a ballad unfortunately incomplete (see p. 140).

Every famous outlaw of English tradition visits the king's court sooner or later, and makes peace with the king; but Robin's independence was too dear to him—and to the ballad-singers whose ideal he was—to allow him to go to the king voluntarily. Therefore the king must come to Robin; and here the compiler, perhaps, saw his opportunity to introduce the king-in-disguise theme, and so evolved the two last fyttes of the *Gest*.

THE EIGHTH FYTTE

> 418.
>
> 'HASTE thou ony grene cloth,' sayd our kynge,
>
> 'That thou wylte sell nowe to me?'

'Ye, for God,' sayd Robyn,

'Thyrty yerdes and three.'

419.

'Robyn,' sayd our kynge,

'Now pray I thee,

Sell me some of that cloth

To me and my meynë.'

420.

'Yes, for God,' then sayd Robyn,

'Or elles I were a fole;

Another day ye wyll me clothe,

I trowe, ayenst the Yole.'

421.

421.[1] 'kest of' = cast off: 'colë,' frock (cp. 372.[1]).

The kynge kest of his colë then,

A grene garment he dyde on,

And every knyght also, i-wys,

Another had full sone.

422.

When they were clothed in Lyncolne grene,

They keste away theyr graye.

'Now we shall to Notyngham,'

All thus our kynge gan say.

423.

423.[1] 'bente,' took.

423.[2] 'in fere,' in company.

They bente theyr bowes, and forth they went,

Shotynge all in fere,

Towarde the towne of Notyngham,

Outlawes as they were.

424.

424.³ 'plucke-buffet,' the game of giving one another alternate buffets, as described in stt. 403-9. In the *Romance of Richard Cœur de Lion*, Richard even kills his opponent at this 'game.' 'Shote plucke-buffet' implies that the buffeting was punishment for missing the mark at shooting.

Our kynge and Robyn rode togyder,

For soth as I you say;

And they shote plucke-buffet,

As they went by the way.

425.

And many a buffet our kynge wan

Of Robyn Hode that day,

And nothynge spared good Robyn

Our kynge in his pay.

426.

'So God me helpë,' sayd our kynge,

'Thy game is nought to lere;

I sholde not get a shote of thee,

Though I shote all this yere.'

427.

All the people of Notyngham

They stode and behelde;

They sawe nothynge but mantels of grene

That covered all the felde.

428.

428.² 'slone,' slain.

Than every man to other gan say,

'I drede our kynge be slone;

Come Robyn Hode to the towne, i-wys

On lyve he lefte never one.'

429.

429.4 'hypped,' hopped.

Full hastëly they began to fle,

Both yemen and knaves,

And olde wyves that myght evyll goo,

They hyppëd on theyr staves.

430.

The kynge loughe full fast,

And commaunded theym agayne;

When they se our comly kynge,

I-wys they were full fayne.

431.

They ete and dranke, and made them glad,

And sange with notës hye;

Than bespake our comly kynge

To Syr Richarde at the Lee.

432.

He gave hym there his londe agayne,

A good man he bad hym be;

Robyn thanked our comly kynge,

And set hym on his kne.

433.

433.4 'fe,' pay.

Had Robyn dwelled in the kyngës courte

But twelve monethes and thre,

That he had spent an hondred pounde,
And all his mennës fe.

434.

434.² 'layde downe,' spent, laid out.
In every place where Robyn came
Ever more he layde downe,
Both for knyghtës and for squyres,
To gete hym grete renowne.

435.

By than the yere was all agone
He had no man but twayne,
Lytell Johan and good Scathelocke,
With hym all for to gone.

436.

Robyn sawe yonge men shote
Full fayre upon a day;
'Alas!' than sayd good Robyn,
'My welthe is went away.

437.

'Somtyme I was an archere good,
A styffe and eke a stronge;
I was compted the best archere
That was in mery Englonde.

438.

438.⁴ 'sloo,' slay.
'Alas!' then sayd good Robyn,
'Alas and well a woo!
Yf I dwele lenger with the kynge,
Sorowe wyll me sloo.'

439.

Forth than went Robyn Hode

Tyll he came to our kynge:

'My lorde the kynge of Englonde,

Graunte me myn askynge.

440.

'I made a chapell in Bernysdale,

That semely is to se,

It is of Mary Magdaleyne,

And thereto wolde I be.

441.

'I myght never in this seven nyght

No tyme to slepe ne wynke,

Nother all these seven dayes

Nother ete ne drynke.

442.

442.³ 'wolwarde,' with wool against skin, *i.e.* with a sheepskin turned inwards: 'hyght,' promised, vowed.

'Me longeth sore to Bernysdale,

I may not be therfro;

Barefote and wolwarde I have hyght

Thyder for to go.'

443.

'Yf it be so,' than sayd our kynge,

'It may no better be;

Seven nyght I gyve thee leve,

No lengre, to dwell fro me.'

444.

'Gramercy, lorde,' then sayd Robyn,

And set hym on his kne;
He toke his leve full courteysly,
To grene wode then went he.

445.
When he came to grene wode,
In a mery mornynge,
There he herde the notës small
Of byrdës mery syngynge.
446.
446.³ 'Me lyste,' I should like.
446.⁴ 'donne,' dun (cf. 417.³).
'It is ferre gone,' sayd Robyn,
'That I was last here;
Me lyste a lytell for to shote
At the donnë dere.'
447.
Robyn slewe a full grete harte;
His horne than gan he blow,
That all the outlawes of that forest
That horne coud they knowe,
448.
448.² 'throwe,' space of time.
448.⁴ See 306.⁴, etc.
And gadred them togyder,
In a lytell throwe.
Seven score of wyght yonge men
Came redy on a rowe,
449.

And fayre dyde of theyr hodes,

And set them on theyr kne:

'Welcome,' they sayd, 'our derë mayster,

Under this grene-wode tre.'

450.

Robyn dwelled in grenë wode

Twenty yere and two;

For all drede of Edwarde our kynge,

Agayne wolde he not goo.

451.

Yet he was begyled, i-wys,

Through a wycked woman,

The pryoresse of Kyrkësly,

That nye was of hys kynne:

452.

452.³ 'speciall,' lover.

452.⁴ Cp. 234.², 349.².

For the love of a knyght,

Syr Roger of Donkesly,

That was her ownë speciall;

Full evyll mote they the!

453.

453.⁴ 'banis,' murderers.

They toke togyder theyr counsell

Robyn Hood for to sle,

And how they myght best do that dede,

His banis for to be.

454.

Than bespake good Robyn,

In place where as he stode,

'Tomorow I muste to Kyrkësly,

Craftely to be leten blode.'

455.

Syr Roger of Donkestere

By the pryoresse he lay,

And there they betrayed good Robyn Hode,

Through theyr falsë playe.

456.

Cryst have mercy on his soul,

That dyëd on the rode!

For he was a good outlawe,

And dyde pore men moch gode.

ROBIN AND GANDELEYN

THE TEXT is modernised from the only known version, in Sloane MS. 2593, in the British Museum (c. 1450); the minstrel's song-book which contains the famous carols: 'I sing of a maiden,' and 'Adam lay i-bounden.' This ballad was first printed by Ritson in his *Ancient Songs* (1790); but he misunderstood the phrase 'Robyn lyth' in the burden for the name 'Robin Lyth,' and ingeniously found a cave on Flamborough Head called Robin Lyth's Hole.

THE STORY is similar to those told of Robin Hood and Little John; but there is no ground for identifying this Robin with Robin Hood. Wright, in printing the Sloane MS., notes that 'Gandeleyn' resembles Gamelyn, whose 'tale' belongs to the pseudo-Chaucerian literature. But we can only take this ballad to be, like so many others, an unrelated 'relique.'

ROBIN AND GANDELEYN

    1.

1.[1] 'carping' = talking, tale.

1.[5] This line is the burden: it is repeated at the end in the MS.

I HEARD a carping of a clerk

All at yon woodës end,

Of good Robin and Gandeleyn,

Was there none other thing.

Robin lieth in greenwood bounden.

    2.

2.[1] 'wern' = were (plural termination as in 'wenten,' etc.); 'children,' young fellows, as in 'Child Roland,' etc.

Strong thievës wern tho children none,

But bowmen good and hend;

They wenten to wood to getten them flesh

If God would it them send.

    3.

All day wenten tho children two,
And flesh founden they none,
Till it were again even,
The children would gone home.
4.
Half a hundred of fat fallow deer
They comen ayon,
And all they wern fair and fat enow,
But markëd was there none.
'By dear God,' said good Robin,
'Hereof we shall have one.'
5.
5.[2] 'flo,' arrow.
Robin bent his jolly bow,
Therein he set a flo;
The fattest deer of all.
The heart he cleft a-two.
6.
6.[1] 'i-flaw' = flayed. Cp. 'slaw,' 16.[3].
He had not the deer i-flaw
Ne half out of the hide,
There came a shrewd arrow out of the west
That felled Robert's pride.

7.
Gandeleyn looked him east and west,
By every side:
'Who hath my master slain?
Who hath done this deed?

Shall I never out of greenwood go

Till I see his sidës bleed.'

8.

8.¹ MS. reads 'and lokyd west.'

8.⁴ 'clepen,' name, call.

Gandeleyn looked him east and west,

And sought under the sun;

He saw a little boy.

They clepen Wrennok of Donne.

9.

A good bow in his hand,

A broad arrow therein,

And four and twenty good arrows

Trussèd in a thrum.

'Beware thee, ware thee, Gandeleyn,

Hereof thou shalt have some.

10.

10.⁴ 'Misaunter [= misadventure] have' was used in imprecations: cf. in the *Merlin* romance, 'Mysauenture haue that it kepeth eny counseile.'

'Beware thee, ware thee, Gandeleyn,

Hereof thou gettest plenty.'

'Ever one for another,' said Gandeleyn;

'Misaunter have they shall flee.

11.

11.³ 'Each at the other's heart.'

'Whereat shall our mark be?'

Saidë Gandeleyn.

'Everich at otherës heart,'

Said Wrennok again.

9.[4] *i.e.*, laced in a thrum, or warp.

12.

'Who shall give the first shot?'

Saidë Gandeleyn.

'And I shall give thee one before,'

Said Wrennok again.

13.

13.[3] 'sanchothes': unexplained; but it obviously means that the arrow struck between his legs.

Wrennok shot a full good shot,

And he shot not too high;

Through the sanchothës of his breek,

It touchëd neither thigh.

14.

'Now hast thou given me one before';

All thus to Wrennok said he;

'And through the might of our Lady

A better I shall give thee.'

15.

Gandeleyn bent his good bow,

And set therein a flo;

He shot through his green kirtle,

His heart he cleft on two.

16.

16.[1] 'yelp,' boast.

16.[3] 'slaw,' slain.

'Now shalt thou never yelp, Wrennok,

At ale ne at wine,

That thou hast slaw good Robin

And his knave Gandeleyn.

17.

'Now shalt thou never yelp, Wrennok,

At wine ne at ale,

That thou hast slaw good Robin

And Gandeleyn his knave.'

ROBIN HOOD AND THE MONK

THE TEXT is modernised from a MS. in the University Library, Cambridge (MS. Ff. v. 48), which belongs to the middle of the fifteenth century. We have also a single leaf of another MS. version, of about the same date, preserved amongst the Bagford Ballads in the British Museum, but this contains a bare half-dozen stanzas.

THE STORY might be called a counterpart to *Robin Hood and Guy of Gisborne*, inasmuch as it has Little John for its hero, and relates how he set his master free, although Robin had lost his temper with him in the morning. A most unfortunate hiatus after 30.[2] prevents us from learning how Robin's fate was reported to his men; but as it stands it is a perfect ballad, straightforward, lively, and picturesque. The first five stanzas, which make a delightful little lyric in themselves, breathe the whole spirit of the greenwood.

ROBIN HOOD AND THE MONK

1.

1.[1] 'shaws,' woods, thickets: 'sheen,' beautiful.

IN summer, when the shaws be sheen
And leaves be large and long,
It is full merry in fair forest
To hear the fowlës song,

2.

2.[2] 'hee,' high. Cf. 84.[2].

To see the deer draw to the dale,
And leave the hillës hee,
And shadow them in the leavës green,
Under the greenwood tree.

3.

3.[3] 'can,' did.

It befel on Whitsuntide,

Early in a May morning,

The sun up fair can shine,

And the briddës merry can sing.

4.

'This is a merry morning,' said Little John,

'By him that died on tree;

A more merry man than I am one

Lives not in Christiantë.

5.

'Pluck up thy heart, my dear master,'

Little John can say,

'And think it is a full fair time

In a morning of May.'

6.

'Yea, one thing grieves me,' said Robin,

'And does my heart much woe;

That I may not no solemn day

To mass nor matins go.

7.

7.[2] *i.e.*, since I took the sacrament.

'It is a fortnight and more,' said he,

'Syn I my Saviour see;

To-day will I to Nottingham,

With the might of mild Marie.'

8.

8.[1] 'milner son,' = miller's son: cp. 24.[3].

8.[5] 'slon,' slay.

Then spake Much the milner son,

Ever more well him betide!
'Take twelve of thy wight yeomen,
Well weapon'd by thy side.
Such one would thyselfë slon,
That twelve dare not abide.'

9.

'Of all my merry men,' said Robin,
'By my faith I will none have,
But Little John shall bear my bow,
Till that me list to draw.'

10.

10.[4] 'lyne,' tree: so 'lynd' in 23.[2]. Cf. 76.[4], 78.[3], etc.

'Thou shall bear thine own,' said Little John,
'Master, and I will bear mine,
And we will shoot a penny,' said Little John,
'Under the greenwood lyne.'

11.

11.[4] *i.e.*, I will give you odds of three to one.

'I will not shoot a penny,' said Robin Hood,
'In faith, Little John, with thee,
But ever for one as thou shootës,' said Robin,
'In faith I hold thee three.'

12.

Thus shot they forth, these yeomen two,
Both at bush and broom,
Till Little John won of his master
Five shillings to hose and shoon.

13.

13.[1] 'ferly,' strange.

A ferly strife fell them between,

As they went by the way,

Little John said he had won five shillings

And Robin Hood said shortly nay.

14.

14.[1] 'lied,' gave the lie to.

With that Robin Hood lied Little John,

And smote him with his hand;

Little John waxëd wroth therewith,

And pulled out his bright brand.

15.

15.[2] 'by,' aby, atone for.

'Were thou not my master,' said Little John,

'Thou shouldest by it full sore;

Get thee a man where thou wilt,

For thou gettest me no more.'

16.

16.[4] 'ilkone' = each one: cf. 30.[2].

Then Robin goes to Nottingham,

Himself mourning alone,

And Little John to merry Sherwood,

The paths he knew ilkone.

17.

17.[2] Another form of 'certain without leasing' = forsooth without lying. Cf. 81.[2].

When Robin came to Nottingham,

Certainly withouten layn,

He prayed to God and mild Mary

To bring him out safe again.

100

18.

He goes into Saint Mary church,

And kneeled down before the rood;

All that ever were the church within,

Beheld well Robin Hood.

19.

Beside him stood a great-headed monk,

I pray to God woe he be!

Full soon he knew good Robin,

As soon as he him see.

20.

20.[4] 'sparred,' shut: 'everychone,' every one (cf. 16.[4]).

Out at the door he ran,

Full soon and anon;

All the gates of Nottingham,

He made to be sparred everychone.

21.

21.[2] *i.e.*, make ready: cf. *Guy of Gisborne*, 5.[1].

'Rise up,' he said, 'thou proud sheriff,

Busk thee, and make thee bown;

I have spied the kingës felon,

For sooth he is in this town.

22.

22.[4] 'And' = if: 'it will be your fault if he escapes us.'

'I have spied the false felon,

As he standës at his mass;

It is long of thee,' said the monk,

'And ever he fro us pass.

23.

23.[1] 'traitor' is genitive: cf. 'milner son,' 8.[1], and 'mother son,' 24.[3].

'This traitor name is Robin Hood,

Under the greenwood lynd;

He robbëd me once of a hundred pound,

It shall never out of my mind.'

24.

24.[2] 'radly,' quickly: 'yare,' ready.

24.[3] See notes 8.[1], 23.[1].

Up then rose this proud sheriff,

And radly made him yare;

Many was the mother son,

To the kirk with him can fare.

25.

25.[1] 'throly thrast,' strenuously pressed.

25.[2] 'wone,' plenty.

In at the doors they throly thrast,

With stavës full good wone;

'Alas, alas!' said Robin Hood,

'Now miss I Little John.'

26.

26.[3] 'Thereas' = where. Cf. 72.[3].

But Robin took out a two-hand sword

That hangëd down by his knee;

Thereas the sheriff and his men stood thickest,

Thitherward would he.

27.

Thrice throughout them he ran then

For sooth as I you say,

And wounded many a mother son,

And twelve he slew that day.

28.

His sword upon the sheriff head

Certainly he brake in two;

'The smith that thee made,' said Robin,

'I pray God work him woe.'

29.

29.³ 'But if' = unless.

'For now am I weaponless,' said Robin,

'Alas! against my will;

But if I may flee these traitors fro,

I wot they will me kill.'

30.

30.² Cf. 16.⁴. Probably six stanzas are lost here.

Robin into the churchë ran,

Throughout them everilkone,

.   .   .   .   .

.   .   .   .   .

31.

Some fell in swooning as they were dead,

And lay still as any stone;

None of them were in their mind

But only Little John.

32.

32.¹ 'rule,' behaviour, conduct.

'Let be your rule,' said Little John,

- 125 -

'For his love that died on tree;
Ye that should be doughty men;
It is great shame to see.
33.
'Our master has been hard bestood,
And yet scapëd away;
Pluck up your hearts and leave this moan,
And hearken what I shall say.
34.
34.² 'securly' = surely.
'He has servëd Our Lady many a day,
And yet will, securly;
Therefore I trust her specially
No wicked death shall he die.

35.
'Therefore be glad,' said Little John,
'And let this mourning be;
And I shall be the monkës guide,
With the might of mild Marie.'
36.

.   .   .   .   .

'We will go but we two;
And I meet him,' said Little John,

.   .   .   .   .

37.
37.¹ 'tristel-tree,' trysting-tree.
'Look that ye keep well our tristel-tree,
Under the leavës smale,

And spare none of this venison

That goës in this vale.'

38.

38.² 'on fere,' in company.

38.³ 'Much emës house,' the house of Much's uncle.

Forth then went these yeomen two,

Little John and Much on fere,

And lookëd on Much emës house,

The highway lay full near.

39.

39.² 'at a stage': ? from an upper story.

Little John stood at a window in the morning,

And lookëd forth at a stage;

He was ware where the monk came riding,

And with him a little page.

40.

'By my faith,' said Little John to Much,

'I can thee tell tidingës good;

I see where the monkë comës riding,

I know him by his wide hood.'

41.

41.² 'hand,' gallant.

41.³ 'spyrrëd . . . at,' asked . . . of. (Cf. Scottish 'speir.')

41.⁴ 'friende' is plural.

They went into the way, these yeomen both,

As curteis men and hend;

They spyrrëd tidingës at the monk,

As they had been his friende.

42.

'Fro whence come ye?' said Little John,

'Tell us tidingës, I you pray,

Of a false outlaw, called Robin Hood,

Was taken yesterday.

43.

'He robbed me and my fellows both

Of twenty mark in certain;

If that false outlaw be taken;

For sooth we would be fain.'

44.

'So did he me,' said the monk,

'Of a hundred pound and more;

I laid first hand him upon,

Ye may thank me therefore.'

45.

'I pray God thank you,' said Little John,

'And we will when we may;

We will go with you, with your leave,

And bring you on your way.

46.

'For Robin Hood has many a wild fellow,

I tell you in certain;

If they wist you rode this way,

In faith ye should be slain.'

47.

As they went talking by the way,

The monk and Little John,

John took the monkës horse by the head,

Full soon and anon.

48.

48.4 'For' = for the purpose that. Cp. 'for' in *Child Waters*, 28.6, First Series, p. 41.

John took the monkës horse by the head,

Forsooth as I you say;

So did Much the little page,

For he should not scape away.

49.

49.3 'of him agast,' afraid of the consequences to him.

By the gullet of the hood

John pulled the monkë down;

John was nothing of him agast,

He let him fall on his crown.

50.

Little John was sore aggrieved,

And drew out his sword on high;

This monkë saw he should be dead,

Loud mercy can he cry.

51.

51.2 'bale,' trouble.

'He was my master,' said Little John,

'That thou hast brought in bale;

Shall thou never come at our king,

For to tell him tale.'

52.

John smote off the monkës head,

No longer would he dwell;

So did Much the little page,

For fear lest he would tell.

53.

There they buriëd them both,
In neither moss nor ling,
And Little John and Much in fere
Bare the letters to our king.

54.

54.⁴ 'see,' protect.

.   .   .   .   .

He kneelëd down upon his knee:
'God you save, my liegë lord,
Jesus you save and see!

55.

'God you save, my liegë king!'
To speak John was full bold;
He gave him the letters in his hand,
The king did it unfold.

56.

56.² Cf. *Gest*, 234.².

The king read the letters anon,
And said, 'So mote I the,
There was never yeoman in merry England
I longëd so sore to see.

57.

57.⁴ 'after': 'by,' as we should say.

'Where is the monk that these should have brought?'
Our king can say:
'By my troth,' said Little John,

'He died after the way.'

58.

The king gave Much and Little John
Twenty pound in certain,
And made them yeomen of the crown,
And bade them go again.

59.

59.[4] 'dere,' injury.

He gave John the seal in hand,
The sheriff for to bear,
To bring Robin him to,
And no man do him dere.

60.

60.[4] 'yede' (= gaed), went.

John took his leave at our king,
The sooth as I you say;
The next way to Nottingham
To take, he yede the way.

61.

61.[2] 'sparred': cp. 20.[4].

When John came to Nottingham
The gatës were sparred each one;
John callëd up the porter,
He answerëd soon anon.

62.

'What is the cause,' said Little John,
'Thou sparrës the gates so fast?'
'Because of Robin Hood,' said the porter,

'In deep prison is cast.

63.

63.⁴ 'sauten,' assault.

'John and Much and Will Scathlock,

For sooth as I you say,

They slew our men upon our wallës,

And sauten us every day.'

64.

64.¹ Cp. 41.³.

Little John spyrred after the sheriff,

And soon he him found;

He opened the kingës privy seal

And gave him in his hond.

65.

When the sheriff saw the kingës seal,

He did off his hood anon;

'Where is the monk that bare the letters?'

He said to Little John.

66.

'He is so fain of him,' said Little John,

'For sooth as I you say,

He has made him abbot of Westminster,

A lord of that abbay.'

67.

The sheriff made John good cheer,

And gave him wine of the best;

At night they went to their bed,

And every man to his rest.

68.

When the sheriff was on sleep,

Drunken of wine and ale,

Little John and Much for sooth

Took the way unto the jail.

69.

Little John callëd up the jailor;

And bade him rise anon;

He said Robin Hood had broken prison,

And out of it was gone.

70.

The porter rose anon certain,

As soon as he heard John call;

Little John was ready with a sword,

And bare him to the wall.

71.

'Now will I be porter,' said Little John,

'And take the keys in hond';

He took the way to Robin Hood,

And soon he him unbound.

72.

He gave him a good sword in his hand,

His head therewith for to keep,

And thereas the wall was lowest

Anon down can they leap.

73.

73.4 'comyn' = commons': *i.e.* the town bell.

By that the cock began to crow,

The day began to spring;

The sheriff found the jailor dead,

The comyn bell made he ring.

74.

74.⁴ 'warison,' reward.

He made a cry throughout all the town,

Whether he be yeoman or knave,

That could bring him Robin Hood,

His warison he should have.

75.

'For I dare never,' said the sheriff,

'Come before our king;

For if I do, I wot certain

For sooth he will me hing.'

76.

76.² 'sty,' alley.

The sheriff made to seek Nottingham,

Both by street and sty,

And Robin was in merry Sherwood,

As light as leaf on lynd.

77.

77.⁴ 'Quite thee,' acquit yoursle, *i.e.* reward me. But the Baford MS. reads 'Quit me.'

Then bespake good Little John,

To Robin Hood can he say,

'I have done thee a good turn for an evil;

Quite thee when thou may.

78.

'I have done thee a good turn,' said Little John,

'For sooth as I you say;

I have brought thee under green wood lyne;

Farewell, and have good day.'

79.

'Nay, by my troth,' said Robin Hood,

'So shall it never be:

I make thee master,' said Robin Hood,

'Of all my men and me.'

80.

80.[4] 'keep I be,' I care to be.

'Nay, by my troth,' said Little John,

'So shall it never be;

But let me be a fellow,' said Little John,

'No nother keep I be.'

81.

81.[4] 'fain,' glad.

Thus John gat Robin Hood out of prison,

Certain withouten layn;

When his men saw him whole and sound,

For sooth they were full fain.

82.

They filled in wine, and made them glad,

Under the leavës smale,

And gat pasties of venison,

That goodë was with ale.

83.

Then wordë came to our king

How Robin Hood was gone,

And how the sheriff of Nottingham

Durst never look him upon.

84.

84.² 'hee': see 2.².

Then bespake our comely king,

In an anger hee:

'Little John has beguiled the sheriff,

In faith so has he me.

85.

'Little John has beguiled us both,

And that full well I see;

Or else the sheriff of Nottingham

High hangëd should he be.

86.

86.³ 'grith,' peace (Norse, 'grið').

'I made them yeomen of the crown,

And gave them fee with my hand;

I gave them grith,' said our king;

'Throughout all merry England.

87.

87.² See 56.².

'I gave them grith,' then said our king;

'I say, so mote I the,

Forsooth such a yeoman as he is one

In all England are not three.

88.

'He is true to his master,' said our king;

'I say, by sweet Saint John,

He lovës better Robin Hood

Than he does us each one.

89.

89.² *i.e.* whether on the road, or housed.

'Robin Hood is ever bound to him,

Both in street and stall;

Speak no more of this matter,' said our king;

'But John has beguiled us all.'

90.

Thus ends the talking of the monk,

And Robin Hood i-wis;

God, that is ever a crownëd king,

Bring us all to his bliss!

ROBIN HOOD AND THE POTTER

THE TEXT is modernised, as far as is possible, from a MS. of about 1500 in the University Library at Cambridge (Ee. 4, 35). The ballad was first printed therefrom by Ritson in his *Robin Hood* (1795), vol. i. p. 81, on the whole very accurately, and with a few necessary emendations. He notes that the scribe was evidently 'a vulgar and illiterate person' who 'irremediably corrupted' the ballad. In several places, however, a little ingenuity will restore a lost rhyme.

THE STORY, of an outlaw disguising himself in order to gain information from his enemies, is common to the legends of Hereward the Saxon, Wallace, Eustace the monk, and Fulk Fitz Warine, the first three of whom assumed the guise of a potter at one time or another.

The ballad of *Robin Hood and the Butcher* is a tale similar to this; and part of the Play of Robin Hood is based on this ballad (see Introduction, p. xxiii.).

ROBIN HOOD AND THE POTTER

1.

IN summer, when the leavës spring,

The blossoms on every bough,

So merry doth the birdës sing

In woodës merry now.

2.

Hearken, good yeomen,

Comely, courteous, and good;

One of the best that ever bare bow,

His name was Robin Hood.

3.

Robin Hood was the yeoman's name,

That was both courteous and free;

For the love of Our Lady

All women worshipped he.

4.

But as the good yeoman stood on a day,
Among his merry meynë,
He was ware of a proud potter
Came driving over the lee.

5.

5.4 'pavage,' road-tax.

'Yonder cometh a proud potter,' said Robin,
'That long hath haunted this way;
He was never so courteous a man
One penny of pavage to pay.'

6.

'I met him but at Wentbridge,' said Little John,
'And therefore evil mote he thee!
Such three strokës he me gave,
That by my sides cleft they.

7.

7.4 'wed,' pledge, wager.

'I lay forty shillings,' said Little John,
'To pay it this same day,
There is not a man among us all
A wed shall make him lay.'

8.

8.2 'and,' if.

'Here is forty shillings,' said Robin,
'More, and thou dare say,
That I shall make that proud potter,
A wed to me shall he lay.'

9.

9.² 'toke,' gave.

9.³ 'breyde,' rushed, leapt.

There this money they laid,

They toke it a yeoman to keep.

Robin before the potter he breyde

And bade him stand still.

10.

Hands upon his horse he laid,

And bade the potter stand full still;

The potter shortly to him said,

'Fellow, what is thy will?'

11.

'All this three year and more, potter,' he said,

'Thou hast haunted this way,

Yet were thou never so courteous a man

One penny of pavage to pay.'

12.

'What is thy name,' said the potter,

''Fore pavage thou ask of me?'

'Robin Hood is my name,

A wed shall thou leave me.'

13.

13.⁴ 'tene,' harm.

'Wed will I none leave,' said the potter,

'Nor pavage will I none pay;

Away thy hand fro my horse!

I will thee tene else, by my fay.'

14.

The potter to his cart he went,

He was not to seek;

A good two-hand staff he hent,

Before Robin he leaped.

15.

Robin out with a sword bent,

A buckler in his hand;

The potter to Robin he went

And said, 'Fellow, let my horse go.'

16.

16.[3] *i.e.* thereat laughed Robin's men.

Together then went these two yeomen,

It was a good sight to see;

Thereof low Robin his men,

There they stood under a tree.

17.

17.[3] 'ackward,' back-handed (?).

Little John to his fellows said,

'Yon potter will stiffly stand':

The potter, with an ackward stroke,

Smote the buckler out of his hand.

18.

18.[4] 'yede,' went.

And ere Robin might get it again

His buckler at his feet,

The potter in the neck him took,

To the ground soon he yede.

19.

19.[4] 'slo,' slay.

That saw Robin his men

As they stood under a bough;

'Let us help our master,' said Little John,

'Yonder potter else will him slo.'

20.

20.[1] 'a breyde,' haste.

These yeomen went with a breyde,

To their master they came.

Little John to his master said

'Who hath the wager won?'

21.

'Shall I have your forty shillings,' said Little John,

'Or ye, master, shall have mine?'

'If they were a hundred,' said Robin,

'I' faith, they been all thine.'

22.

22.[4] 'let,' stop, hinder.

'It is full little courtesy,' said the potter,

'As I have heard wise men say,

If a poor yeoman come driving on the way

To let him of his journey.'

23.

23.[3] 'And,' if.

'By my troth, thou says sooth,' said Robin,

'Thou says good yeomanry;

And thou drive forth every day,

Thou shalt never be let for me.

24.

'I will pray thee, good potter,

A fellowship will thou have?

Give me thy clothing, and thou shalt have mine;

I will go to Nottingham.'

25.

25.³ 'But,' unless.

25.⁴ 'yode,' went.

'I grant thereto,' said the potter;

'Thou shalt find me a fellow good;

But thou can sell my pottës well,

Come again as thou yode.'

26.

'Nay, by my troth,' said Robin,

'And then I beshrew my head,

If I bring any pottës again,

And any wife will them chepe.'

27.

Then spake Little John,

And all his fellows hend;

'Master, be well ware of the sheriff of Nottingham,

For he is little our friend.'

28.

28.¹ 'Heyt war howt,' a call to horses while driving, like the modern 'Gee up.'

'Heyt war howt,' said Robin;

'Fellows, let me alone;

Through the help of Our Lady,

To Nottingham will I gone.'

29.

Robin went to Nottingham,

These pottës for to sell;

The potter abode with Robin's men,

There he fared not ill.

30.

Though Robin drove on his way,

So merry over the land:

Here is more, and after is to say

The best is behind.

31.

When Robin came to Nottingham,

The sooth if I should say,

He set up his horse anon,

And gave him oats and hay.

26.[4] 'chepe,' bargain for, buy.

32.

32.[4] 'hansel' is a gift, especially an 'earnest' or instalment; 'mare' probably is 'more'; but the meaning of the whole phrase is uncertain.

In the midst of the town,

There he showed his ware;

'Pottës, pottës,' he gan cry full soon,

'Have hansel for the mare!'

33.

33.[2] 'chaffare,' merchandise.

Full often against the sheriff's gate

Showëd he his chaffare;

Wives and widows about him drew

- 144 -

And chepëd fast of his ware.

34.

34.[1] 'great chepe' = great bargain.

Yet, 'Pottës, great chepe!' cried Robin,
'I love evil thus to stand.'
And all that saw him sell
Said he had be no potter long.

35.

35.[4] 'thee,' thrive.

The pottës that were worth pence five,
He sold them for pence three;
Privily said man and wife,
'Yonder potter shall never thee.'

36.

Thus Robin sold full fast,
Till he had pottës but five;
Up he them took off his car
And sent them to the sheriff's wife.

37.

37.[1] 'fain,' glad.

Thereof she was full fain;
'Gramercy, sir,' then said she;
'When ye come to this country again
I shall buy of thy pottës, so mote I thee.'

38.

'Ye shall have of the best,' said Robin,
And sware by the Trinity;
Full courteously she gan him call,

'Come dine with the sheriff and me.'

39.

'God amercy,' said Robin,

'Your bidding shall be done.'

A maiden in the pottës gan bear,

Robin and the sheriff wife followed anon.

40.

40.[3] 'could of courtesy,' knew how to be courteous.

40.[4] 'gret,' greeted.

When Robin into the hall came,

The sheriff soon he met;

The potter could of courtesy,

And soon the sheriff he gret.

41.

'Lo, sir, what this potter hath give you and me;

Five pottës small and great!'

'He is full welcome,' said the sheriff,

'Let us wash, and go to meat.'

42.

As they sat at their meat,

With a noble cheer,

Two of the sheriff's men gan speak

Of a great wager;

43.

Of a shooting was good and fine,

Was made the other day,

Of forty shillings, the sooth to say,

Who should this wager win.

44.

Still then sat this proud potter,

Thus then thought he;

'As I am a true Christian man,

This shooting will I see.'

45.

45.³ 'prest,' quickly.

When they had fared of the best,

With bread, and ale, and wine,

To the butts they made them prest,

With bows and bolts full fine.

46.

The sheriff's men shot full fast,

As archers that were good;

There came none near nigh the mark

By half a good archer's bow.

47.

47.³ 'And,' if.

Still then stood the proud potter,

Thus then said he;

'And I had a bow, by the rood,

One shot should ye see.'

48.

'Thou shall have a bow,' said the sheriff,

'The best that thou will choose of three;

Thou seemest a stalwart and a strong,

Assay[ed] shall thou be.'

49.

The sheriff commanded a yeoman that stood them by,

After bows to wend;

The best bow that the yeoman brought,

Robin set on a string.

50.

'Now shall I wot and thou be good,

And pull it up to thine ear.'

'So God me help,' said the proud potter,

'This is but right weak gear.'

51.

To a quiver Robin went,

A good bolt out he took;

So nigh unto the mark he went,

He failëd not a foot.

52.

All they shot about again,

The sheriff's men and he;

Of the mark he would not fail,

He cleft the prick in three.

53.

The sheriff's men thought great shame

The potter the mastery won;

The sheriff laughed and made good game,

And said, 'Potter, thou art a man.

54.

54.[1,2] Two lines missing in the MS.; so 57.[3].

.   .   .   .   .

.   .   .   .   .

'Thou art worthy to bear a bow

In what place that thou go.'

55.

'In my cart I have a bow,

Forsooth,' he said, 'and that a good;

In my cart is the bow

That gave me Robin Hood.'

56.

'Knowest thou Robin Hood?' said the sheriff;

'Potter, I pray thee tell thou me.'

'A hundred turn I have shot with him,

Under his trystell-tree.'

57.

'I had liefer nor a hundred pound,' said the sheriff,

And sware by the Trinity,

'.   .   .   .   .

That the false outlaw stood by me.'

58.

58.[1] 'rede,' advice.

'And ye will do after my rede,' said the potter,

'And boldly go with me,

And tomorrow, ere we eat bread,

Robin Hood will we see.'

59.

59.[1] 'quite' = requite.

59.[4] 'dight,' prepared.

'I will quite thee,' quoth the sheriff,

'I swear by God of might.'

Shooting they left and home they went,

Their supper was ready dight.

60.

60.² 'busked,' made ready.

60.³ 'ray' = array.

Upon the morrow, when it was day,

He busked him forth to ride;

The potter his cart forth gan ray,

And would not leave behind.

61.

He took leave of the sherriff's wife,

And thanked her of all thing:

'Dame, for my love and you will this wear,

I give you here a gold ring.'

62.

62.² 'yield it thee,' reward thee for it.

'Gramercy,' said the wife,

'Sir, God yield it thee.'

The sheriff's heart was never so light,

The fair forest to see.

63.

63.³ 'prest,' freely.

And when he came into the forest,

Under the leavës green,

Birdës there sang on boughës prest,

It was great joy to see.

64.

64.³ 'awit': either = wit, know, or = await.

'Here it is merry to be,' said Robin,

'For a man that had ought to spend;

By my horn I shall awit

If Robin Hood be here.'

65.

Robin set his horn to his mouth,

And blew a blast that was full good;

That heard his men that there stood,

Far down in the wood.

66.

66.2,3 Two lines omitted in the MS.

66.4 'wood,' mad.

'I hear my master blow,' said Little John,

.   .   .   .   .

.   .   .   .   .

They ran as they were wood.

67.

When they to their master came,

Little John would not spare;

'Master, how have you fare in Nottingham?

How have you sold your ware?'

68.

'Yea, by my troth, Little John,

Look thou take no care;

I have brought the sheriff of Nottingham,

For all our chaffare.'

69.

'He is full welcome,' said Little John,

'This tiding is full good.'

The sheriff had liefer nor a hundred pound

He had never seen Robin Hood.

70.

'Had I wist that before,

At Nottingham when we were,

Thou should not come in fair forest

Of all this thousand year.'

71.

'That wot I well,' said Robin,

'I thank God that ye be here;

Therefore shall ye leave your horse with us

And all your other gear.'

72.

72.[1] A duplicated deprecation: 'I protest—God forbid!'

72.[3,4] Two lines omitted in the MS.; so 74.[3,4].

'That fend I god's forbode,' quoth the sheriff,

So to loose my good;

.   .   .   .   .

.   .   .   .   .

73.

'Hither ye came on horse full high,

And home shall ye go on foot;

And greet well thy wife at home,

The woman is full good.

74.

'I shall her send a white palfrey,

It ambleth, by my fay,

.   .   .   .   .

. . . .

75.

75.³ 'Nere' = ne were, were it not.

'I shall her send a white palfrey,

It ambleth as the wind;

Nere for the love of your wife,

Of more sorrow should you sing!'

76.

Thus parted Robin Hood and the sheriff;

To Nottingham he took the way;

His wife fair welcomed him home,

And to him gan she say:

77.

'Sir, how have you fared in green forest?

Have ye brought Robin home?'

'Dame, the devil speed him, both body and bone;

I have had a full great scorn.

78.

'Of all the good that I have led to green wood,

He hath take it fro me;

All but this fair palfrey,

That he hath sent to thee.'

79.

With that she took up a loud laughing,

And sware by him that died on tree,

'Now have you paid for all the pottës

That Robin gave to me.

80.

'Now ye be come home to Nottingham,

Ye shall have good enow.'

Now speak we of Robin Hood,

And of the potter under the green bough.

81.

'Potter, what was thy pottës worth

To Nottingham that I led with me?'

'They were worth two nobles,' said he,

'So mote I thrive or thee;

So could I have had for them

And I had there be.'

82.

'Thou shalt have ten pound,' said Robin,

'Of money fair and free;

And ever when thou comest to green wood,

Welcome, potter, to me.'

83.

Thus parted Robin, the sheriff, and the potter,

Underneath the green wood tree;

God have mercy on Robin Hood's soul,

And save all good yeomanry!

ROBIN HOOD AND GUY OF GISBORNE

THE TEXT.—The only text of this ballad is in the Percy Folio, from which it is here rendered in modern spelling. Although the original is written continuously, it is almost impossible not to suspect an omission after 2.². Child points out, however, that the abrupt transition is found in other ballads (see *Adam Bell*, 2.²), and Hales and Furnivall put 2.³,⁴ in inverted commas as part of Robin's relation of his dream. Percy's emendation was:

> 'The woodweete sang, and wold not cese,
>
> Sitting upon the spraye,
>
> Soe lowde, he wakend Robin Hood
>
> In the greenwood where he lay.
>
> Now by my faye, said jollye Robin,
>
> A sweaven1 I had this night;
>
> I dreamt me of tow mighty yemen
>
> That fast with me can fight.'

THE STORY.—Whether verses have been lost or not, the story has become confused, as there is nothing to show how Robin knows that the Sheriff of Nottingham holds Little John captive; yet he makes careful preparations to pass himself off as Sir Guy, in order to set John free.

There has come down to us a fragment of a play of Robin Hood and the Sheriff.2 In this dramatic fragment, an unnamed knight is promised a reward by the sheriff if he takes Robin Hood. The knight and Robin shoot and wrestle and fight; Robin wins, cuts off the knight's head, puts on his clothes, and takes the head away with him. A second scene shows how the sheriff takes prisoner the other outlaws, amongst whom is Friar Tuck; but the allocation of the parts in the dialogue is mostly conjectural.

   1. *sweaven*, dream.

   2. See Introduction, p. xxii.

ROBIN HOOD AND GUY OF GISBORNE

   1.

   1.¹ 'shaws,' woods: 'sheen,' beautiful: 'shradds,' copses.

- 155 -

WHEN shaws been sheen, and shradds full fair,

And leaves both large and long,

It is merry, walking in the fair forest,

To hear the small bird's song.

2.

2.[1] 'woodweel,' a small warbler. Percy, Ritson, Hazlitt, Halliwell, Child, Murray, Hales, and Furnivall, have variously identified it with the woodpecker, woodlark, redbreast, greenfinch, nuthatch, and 'golden ouzle.'

The woodweel sang, and would not cease,

Amongst the leaves o' lyne,

And it is by two wight yeomen,

By dear God, that I mean.

.   .   .   .   .

3.

2.[2] 'lyne,' tree.

3.[4] 'wroken,' avenged.

'Methought they did me beat and bind,

And took my bow me fro;

If I be Robin alive in this land,

I'll be wroken on both them two.'

4.

4.[1] 'swevens,' dreams.

'Swevens are swift, master,' quoth John,

'As the wind that blows o'er a hill;

For if it be never so loud this night,

Tomorrow it may be still.'

5.

5.[1] 'Busk ye, bown ye' = get ready.

'Busk ye, bown ye, my merry men all,
For John shall go with me;
For I'll go seek yond wight yeomen
In greenwood where they be.'

6.

They cast on their gown of green,
A shooting gone are they,
Until they came to the merry greenwood,
Where they had gladdest be;
There were they 'ware of a wight yeoman,
His body leaned to a tree.

7.

7.³ 'capul-hide,' horse-skin.

A sword and a dagger he wore by his side,
Had been many a man's bane,
And he was clad in his capul-hide,
Top and tail and mane.

8.

'Stand you still, master,' quoth Little John,
'Under this trusty tree,
And I will go to yond wight yeoman,
To know his meaning truly.'

9.

'Ah, John, by me thou sets no store,
And that's a ferly thing;
How oft send I my men before,
And tarry myself behind?

10.

10.² 'And' = if. So in next line.

'It is no cunning a knave to ken,

And a man but hear him speak;

And it were not for bursting of my bow,

John, I would thy head break.'

11.

But often words they breeden bale;

That parted Robin and John;

John is gone to Barnësdale,

The gates he knows each one.

12.

12.⁴ 'slade,' valley, ravine.

And when he came to Barnësdale,

Great heaviness there he had;

He found two of his fellows

Were slain both in a slade,

13.

And Scarlet afoot flying was,

Over stocks and stone,

For the sheriff with seven score men

Fast after him is gone.

14.

'Yet one shot I'll shoot,' says Little John,

'With Christ his might and main;

I'll make yond fellow that flies so fast

To be both glad and fain.'

15.

15.² 'fettled,' prepared.

John bent up a good yew bow,

And fettled him to shoot;
The bow was made of a tender bough,
And fell down to his foot.

16.

16.3,4 'bale, boot,' trouble, help.

'Woe worth thee, wicked wood,' said Little John,
'That e'er thou grew on a tree!
For this day thou art my bale,
My boot when thou should be.'

17.

This shot it was but loosely shot,
The arrow flew in vain,
And it met one of the sheriff's men;
Good William a Trent was slain.

18.

It had been better for William a Trent
To hang upon a gallow
Than for to lie in the greenwood,
There slain with an arrow.

19.

And it is said, when men be met,
Six can do more than three:
And they have ta'en Little John,
And bound him fast to a tree.

20.

20.1 'quoth the sheriff' is added in the MS.

'Thou shalt be drawn by dale and down,
And hanged high on a hill.'

'But thou may fail,' quoth Little John,

'If it be Christ's own will.'

21.

Let us leave talking of Little John,

For he is bound fast to a tree,

And talk of Guy and Robin Hood

In the greenwood where they be;

22.

22.[2] See 2.[2] and 33.[2], where it is obviously a commonplace.

How these two yeomen together they met,

Under the leaves of lyne,

To see what merchandise they made

Even at that same time.

23.

'Good morrow, good fellow,' quoth Sir Guy;

'Good morrow, good fellow,' quoth he;

'Methinks by this bow thou bears in thy hand,

A good archer thou seems to be.

24.

24.[1,2] Sir Guy means he has lost his way, and does not know the time of day.

'I am wilful of my way,' quoth Sir Guy,

'And of my morning tide.'

'I'll lead thee through the wood,' quoth Robin,

'Good fellow, I'll be thy guide.'

25.

'I seek an outlaw,' quoth Sir Guy,

'Men call him Robin Hood;

I had rathèr meet with him upon a day

Than forty pound of gold.'

26.

26.¹ 'whether' = which of the two. Robin, of course, is speaking.

'If you two met, it would be seen whether were better

Afore ye did part away;

Let us some other pastime find,

Good fellow, I thee pray.

27.

27.¹ 'masteries,' feats of skill.

27.⁴ 'unset Steven,' unfixed time: *i.e.* by chance.

'Let us some other masteries make,

And we will walk in the woods even;

We may chance meet with Robin Hood

At some unset steven.'

28.

28.¹ 'shroggy,' wands, sticks.

28.⁴ 'pricks,' marks for shooting at.

They cut them down the summer shroggs

Which grew both under a briar,

And set them three score rood in twain,

To shoot the pricks full near.

29.

'Lead on, good fellow,' said Sir Guy,

'Lead on, I do bid thee.'

'Nay by my faith,' quoth Robin Hood,

'The leader thou shalt be.'

30.

The first good shot that Robin led,

Did not shoot an inch the prick fro;

Guy was an archer good enough,

But he could ne'er shoot so.

31.

31.2,4 The 'garland' was simply a circular wreath, hung upon the 'prick-wand,' or upright stick.

The second shot Sir Guy shot,

He shot within the garland;

But Robin Hood shot it better than he,

For he clove the good prick-wand.

32.

'God's blessing on thy heart!' says Guy,

'Good fellow, thy shooting is good;

For an thy heart be as good as thy hands,

Thou were better than Robin Hood.

33.

'Tell me thy name, good fellow,' quoth Guy,

Under the leaves of lyne:

'Nay, by my faith,' quoth good Robin,

'Till thou have told me thine.'

34.

'I dwell by dale and down,' quoth Guy,

'And I have done many a curst turn;

And he that calls me by my right name

Calls me Guy of good Gisborne.'

35.

35.2 'set by' = care for.

'My dwelling is in the wood,' says Robin;

'By thee I set right nought;

My name is Robin Hood of Barnesdale,

A fellow thou hast long sought.'

36.

36.[4] 'brown': see *Glossary of Ballad Commonplaces*, First Series, p. xlix.

He that had neither been kith nor kin

Might have seen a full fair sight,

To see how together these yeomen went,

With blades both brown and bright;

37.

To have seen how these yeomen together fought

Two hours of a summer's day;

It, was neither Guy nor Robin Hood

That fettled them to fly away.

38.

38.[1] 'reckless on,' heedless of.

Robin was reckless on a root,

And stumbled at that tide,

And Guy was quick and nimble withal,

And hit him o'er the left side.

39.

'Ah, dear Lady!' said Robin Hood,

'Thou art both mother and may!

I think it was never man's destiny

To die before his day.'

40.

40.[3] 'awkward,' unexpected: another ballad-commonplace.

Robin thought on Our Lady dear,

And soon leapt up again,

And thus he came with an awkward stroke;

Good Sir Guy he has slain.

41.

He took Sir Guy's head by the hair,

And sticked it on his bow's end:

'Thou hast been traitor all thy life,

Which thing must have an end.'

42.

42.³ 'That' = so that.

Robin pulled forth an Irish knife,

And nicked Sir Guy in the face,

That he was never on a woman born

Could tell who Sir Guy was.

43.

Says, 'Lie there, lie there, good Sir Guy,

And with me be not wroth;

If thou have had the worse strokes at my hand,

Thou shalt have the better cloth.'

44.

Robin did off his gown of green,

Sir Guy he did it throw;

And he put on that capul-hide

That clad him top to toe.

45.

45.⁴ We are not told how Robin knew what his men were doing.

'The bow, the arrows, and little horn,

And with me now I'll bear;

For now I will go to Barnësdale,

To see how my men do fare.'

46.

46.⁴ 'low,' hill.

Robin set Guy's horn to his mouth,
A loud blast in it he did blow;
That beheard the sheriff of Nottingham,
As he leaned under a low.

47.

'Hearken! hearken!' said the sheriff,
'I heard no tidings but good;
For yonder I hear Sir Guy's horn blow,
For he hath slain Robin Hood.'

48.

'For yonder I hear Sir Guy's horn blow,
It blows so well in tide,
For yonder comes that wighty yeoman,
Clad in his capul-hide.

49.

'Come hither, thou good Sir Guy,
Ask of me what thou wilt have':
'I'll none of thy gold,' says Robin Hood,
'Nor I'll none of it have.'

50.

'But now I have slain the master,' he said,
'Let me go strike the knave;
This is all the reward I ask,
Nor no other will I have.'

51.

'Thou art a madman,' said the sheriff,

'Thou shouldest have had a knight's fee;

Seeing thy asking hath been so bad,

Well granted it shall be.'

52.

52.² 'steven,' voice.

But Little John heard his master speak,

Well he knew that was his steven;

'Now shall I be loosed,' quoth Little John,

'With Christ's might in heaven.'

53.

53.² 'belive,' forthwith.

But Robin he hied him towards Little John,

He thought he would loose him belive;

The sheriff and all his company

Fast after him did drive.

54.

'Stand aback! stand aback!' said Robin;

'Why draw you me so near?

It was never the use in our country

One's shrift another should hear.'

55.

But Robin pulled forth an Irish knife,

And loosed John hand and foot,

And gave him Sir Guy's bow in his hand,

And bade it be his boot.

56.

56.² 'rawsty by the root.' It is suggested that this means rusty (*i.e.* with blood) at the root (tip, end).

But John took Guy's bow in his hand

(His arrows were rawsty by the root);
The sheriff saw Little John draw a bow
And fettle him to shoot.

57.
Towards his house in Nottingham
He fled full fast away,
And so did all his company,
Not one behind did stay.
58.
But he could neither so fast go,
Nor away so fast run,
But Little John, with an arrow broad,
Did cleave his heart in twain.

ROBIN HOOD'S DEATH

THE TEXT is modernised from the Percy Folio MS. (c. 1650). At two points, after 8.³ and 18.², half a page of the MS., or about nine stanzas, is missing—torn out and 'used by maids to light the fire' in Humphry Pitt's house, where Percy discovered the volume (see Introduction, First Series, xxxix.). At the end another half-page is lacking, but Child thinks that it represents only a few verses. He also indicates a lacuna after st. 4, though none appears in the MS.

THE STORY of this version, mutilated as it is, agrees in its main incidents with that given at the end of the *Gest* (stt. 451-455). Another variant, *Robin Hood's Death and Burial*, extant in two or three eighteenth-century 'Garlands,' but none the less of good derivation, gives no assistance at either hiatus, and we are left with a couple of puzzles.

The opening of the ballad, stt. 1-6, should be compared with *Robin Hood and the Monk*, stt. 6-10, where Much takes Will Scarlett's place. Robin, shooting for a penny with Little John along the way, comes to a black water with a plank across it, and an old woman on the plank is cursing Robin Hood. He has been already reminded by Scarlett that he has a yeoman foe at Kirklees; but neither the banning of the witch, nor the weeping of others ('We,' 9.³), presumably women, deter him. The explanation of the witch is lost.

Having arrived at Kirklees and submitted to being bled, Robin at length suspects treason, and hints as much to Little John. The latter may be indoors with his master, or, as Child thinks, calling to Robin through a window from below. Here the second hiatus occurs; and when the ballad resumes, we can only guess that st. 19 is Robin's final retort after an altercation with somebody, presumably Red Roger, who is perhaps the 'yeoman' referred to by Will Scarlett. A final difficulty is raised by the word 'mood' in st. 23; but Child's emendation is not improbable, and Robin himself realises that he must take his 'housel' in an irregular way.

In the Garland version Robin goes alone to Kirklees, where his 'cousin' bleeds him, and leaves him to bleed all day and all night in a locked room. He summons Little John with 'weak blasts three' of his horn, and bids him dig a grave where the last arrow shot by Robin Hood falls.

ROBIN HOOD'S DEATH

    1.

'I WILL never eat nor drink,' Robin Hood said,

'Nor meat will do me no good,

Till I have been at merry Churchlees,

My veins for to let blood.'

2.

2.[1] 'rede,' advise.

'That I rede not,' said Will Scarlett,

'Master, by the assent of me,

Without half a hundred of your best bowmen

You take to go with ye.

3.

'For there a good yeoman doth abide,

Will be sure to quarrel with thee,

And if thou have need of us, master,

In faith we will not flee.'

4.

4.[1,3] 'And,' if.

4.[4] 'A stanza or more seems to be lost here.' —CHILD. There is, however, no break in the MS.

'And thou be fear'd, thou William Scarlett,

At home I rede thee be.'

'And you be wroth, my dear master,

You shall never hear more of me.'

.   .   .   .   .

5.

'For there shall no man with me go,

Nor man with me ride,

And Little John shall be my man,

And bear my benbow by my side.'

6.

6.¹ 'You'st' = you shall.

'You'st bear your bow, master, yourself,

And shoot for a penny with me.'

'To that I do assent,' Robin Hood said,

'And so, John, let it be.'

7.

They two bold children shotten together,

All day theirself in rank,

Until they came to black water,

And over it laid a plank.

8.

8.² 'banning,' cursing.

Upon it there kneeled an old woman,

Was banning Robin Hood,

'Why dost thou ban Robin Hood?' said Robin,

. . . . .

9.

. . . . .

To give to Robin Hood;

We weepen for his dear body,

That this day must be let blood.'

10.

'The dame prior is my aunt's daughter,

And nigh unto my kin;

I know she would me no harm this day,

For all the world to win.'

11.

11.² 'lin,' stop.

Forth then shotten these children two,

And they did never lin,

Until they came to merry Churchlees,

To merry Churchlees within.

12.

And when they came to merry Churchlees,

They knocked upon a pin;

Up then rose dame prioress,

And let good Robin in.

13.

Then Robin gave to dame prioress

Twenty pound in gold,

And bade her spend while that would last,

And she should have more when she wold.

14.

14.² 'in that ilk' [time], at that same moment.

14.³ 'blood-irons,' lancets for bleeding.

And down then came dame prioress,

Down she came in that ilk,

With a pair of blood-irons in her hands,

Were wrappëd all in silk.

15.

'Set a chafing-dish to the fire,' said dame prioress,

'And strip thou up thy sleeve!'

I hold him but an unwise man

That will no warning 'lieve.

16.

She laid the blood-irons to Robin Hood's vein,

Alack, the more pity!

And pierced the vein, and let out the blood,

That full red was to see.

17.

And first it bled the thick, thick blood,

And afterwards the thin,

And well then wist good Robin Hood

Treason there was within.

18.

'What cheer, my master?' said Little John;

'In faith, Little John, little good;

. . . . .

. . . . .

* * * * *

19.

'I have upon a gown of green,

Is cut short by my knee,

And in my hand a bright brown brand

That will well bite of thee.'

20.

20.³ 'glaive,' a sword or knife tied to the end of a pole.

But forth then of a shot-window,

Good Robin Hood he could glide;

Red Roger, with a grounden glaive,

Thrust him through the milk-white side.

21.

But Robin was light and nimble of foot,

And thought to abate his pride,

For between his head and his shoulders

He made a wound full wide.

22.

22.³ 'housel,' communion, sacrament.

Says, 'Lie there, lie there, Red Roger,

The dogs they must thee eat;

For I may have my housel,' he said,

'For I may both go and speak.

23.

23.¹ 'give me mood': Child suggests 'give me my God,' *i.e.* the consecrated Host. He admits it is a bold emendation, but cites some striking parallels in support of it.

'Now give me mood,' Robin said to Little John,

'Give me mood with thy hand;

I trust to God in heaven so high

My housel will me bestand.'

24.

23.⁴ 'bestand,' help.

'Now give me leave, give me leave, master,' he said,

'For Christ's love give leave to me

To set a fire within this hall,

And to burn up all Churchlee.'

25.

'That I rede not,' said Robin Hood then,

'Little John, for it may not be;

If I should do any widow hurt, at my latter end,

God,' he said, 'would blame me;

26.

26.[4] 'greet,' grit, sand.

'But take me upon thy back, Little John,
And bear me to yonder street,
And there make me a full fair grave
Of gravel and of greet.

27.

27.[4] 'met-yard,' measuring-rod.

And set my bright sword at my head,
Mine arrows at my feet,
And lay my yew-bow by my side,
My met-yard wi . . .'

ADAM BELL, CLYM OF THE CLOUGH AND WILLIAM OF CLOUDESLY

THE TEXT.—The earliest complete text, here given, was printed by William Copland between 1548 and 1568: there are extant two printed fragments, one printed by John Byddell in 1536, and the other in a type older than Copland's. Later, there are two editions printed by James Roberts in 1605; and finally a MS. text in the Percy Folio (c. 1650).

Copland's text is obviously full of faults, and in emendations I have mostly followed Child.

THE STORY, lively and admirably told, contains little extrinsic interest, except in William's feat of shooting the apple from his son's head. This is inevitably associated with the legend of William Tell, which is told in the White Book of Obwalden, written about 1470; but similar stories can be found in the Icelandic Saga of Dietrich of Bern (about 1250) and in Saxo Grammaticus, who wrote his Danish History about the year 1200. Three or four other versions of the story are to be found in German and Scandinavian literature before the date of our ballad; but they all agree in two points which are missing in the English ballad—the shot is compulsory, and the archer reserves another arrow for purposes of revenge in case he misses his mark. William of Cloudesly volunteers a difficult and risky feat out of bravado.

The rescue of Cloudesly by Adam Bell and Clym of the Clough may be compared with the rescue of Robin Hood by Little John and Much in *Robin Hood and the Monk*, stt. 61-81 (see pp. 107-110).

ADAM BELL, CLYM OF THE CLOUGH AND WILLIAM OF CLOUDESLY

1.

MERY it was in grene forest

Among the levës grene,

Wher that men walke both east and west

Wyth bowes and arrowes kene;

2.

To ryse the dere out of theyr denne;

Suche sightes as hath ofte bene sene,

As by thre yemen of the north countrey,

By them it is as I meane.

3.

The one of them hight Adam Bel,

The other Clym of the Clough,

The thyrd was William of Cloudesly,

An archer good ynough.

4.

4.[4] 'Englyshe-wood,' Inglewood, reaching from Carlisle to Penrith, in Cumberland.

They were outlawed for venyson,

These thre yemen everychone;

They swore them brethren upon a day,

To Englyshe-wood for to gone.

5.

5.[1] 'lith,' hearken.

Now lith and lysten, gentylmen,

And that of myrthes loveth to here;

Two of them were single men,

The third had a wedded fere.

6.

Wyllyam was the wedded man,

Muche more then was hys care:

He sayde to hys brethren upon a day,

To Carlile he would fare,

7.

For to speke with fayre Alyce his wife,

And with hys chyldren thre:

'By my trouth,' sayde Adam Bel,

'Not by the counsell of me:

8.

'For if ye go to Carlile, brother,
And from thys wylde wode wende,
If that the justice may you take,
Your lyfe were at an ende.'

9.

9.² 'pryme,' about 9 a.m. Cp. 72.².

'If that I come not to-morrowe, brother,
By pryme to you agayne,
Truste not els but that I am take,
Or else that I am slayne.'

10.

He toke hys leave of hys brethren two,
And to Carlel he is gone;
There he knocked at his owne windowe
Shortlye and anone.

11.

'Wher be you, fayre Alyce, my wyfe,
And my chyldren three?
Lyghtly let in thyne husbande,
Wyllyam of Cloudeslee.'

12.

'Alas!' then sayde fayre Alyce,
And syghed wonderous sore,
'Thys place hath ben besette for you
Thys halfe yere and more.'

13.

'Now am I here,' sayde Cloudeslee,

'I would that in I were.

Now feche us meate and drynke ynough,

And let us make good chere.'

14.

She feched hym meate and drynke plenty,

Lyke a true wedded wyfe;

And pleased hym with that she had,

Whome she loved as her lyfe.

15.

15.³ 'found,' provided for.

There lay an old wyfe in that place,

A lytle besyde the fyre,

Whych Wyllyam had found of cherytye

More then seven yere.

16.

Up she rose, and walked full still,

Evel mote shee spede therfore!

For she had not set no fote on ground

In seven yere before.

17.

She went unto the justice hall,

As fast as she could hye:

'Thys night is come unto this town

Wyllyam of Cloudesle.'

18.

18.⁴ 'meed,' reward.

Thereof the justice was full fayne,

And so was the shirife also:

'Thou shalt not travaile hither, dame, for nought,

Thy meed thou shalt have er thou go.'

19.

They gave to her a ryght good goune,

Of scarlat it was, as I heard sayne;

She toke the gyft, and home she wente,

And couched her doune agayne.

20.

They rysed the towne of mery Carlel,

In all the hast that they can;

And came thronging to Wyllyames house,

As fast as they might gone.

21.

There they besette that good yeman

Round about on every syde:

Wyllyam hearde great noyse of folkes,

That heyther-ward they hyed.

22.

Alyce opened a shot-windowe,

And lokëd all aboute,

She was ware of the justice and the shirife bothe,

Wyth a full great route.

23.

'Alas! treason,' cryed Alyce,

'Ever wo may thou be!

Goe into my chamber, my husband,' she sayd,

'Swete Wyllyam of Cloudesle.'

24.

He toke his sweard and hys bucler,

Hys bow and hys chyldren thre,

And wente into hys strongest chamber,

Where he thought surest to be.

25.

Fayre Alyce followed him as a lover true,

With a pollaxe in her hande:

'He shall be deade that here cometh in

Thys dore, while I may stand.'

26.

26.⁴ 'brest,' burst, was broken.

Cloudeslee bente a wel good bowe,

That was of trusty tre,

He smot the justise on the brest,

That hys arowe brest in thre.

27.

'God's curse on his hart,' saide William,

'Thys day thy cote dyd on!

If it had ben no better then myne,

It had gone nere thy bone.'

28.

'Yelde thee, Cloudesle,' sayd the justise,

'And thy bowe and thy arrowes the fro.'

'God's curse on hys hart,' sayd fair Alyce,

'That my husband councelleth so.'

29.

29.³ 'brenne,' burn.

'Set fyre on the house,' saide the sherife,

'Syth it wyll no better be,
And brenne we therin William,' he saide,
'Hys wyfe and chyldren thre.'

30.

They fyred the house in many a place,
The fyre flew up on hye:
'Alas!' than cryed fayr Alice.
'I se we shall here dye.'

31.

William openyd hys backe wyndow,
That was in hys chamber on hie,
And with sheetes let hys wyfe downe
And hys children three.

32.

32.[4] 'wreke,' avenge.

'Have here my treasure,' sayde William,
'My wyfe and my chyldren thre:
For Christës love do them no harme,
But wreke you all on me.'

33.

Wyllyam shot so wonderous well,
Tyll hys arrowes were all go,
And the fyre so fast upon hym fell,
That hys bowstryng brent in two.

34.

The spercles brent and fell hym on,
Good Wyllyam of Cloudesle;
But than was he a wofull man, and sayde,

'Thys is a cowardes death to me.

35.

35.¹ 'Lever,' rather.

35.² 'renne,' run.

35.³ 'wode,' fierce.

'Lever I had,' sayde Wyllyam,

'With my sworde in the route to renne,

Then here among myne enemyes wode

Thus cruelly to bren.'

36.

36.³ 'in prece,' in a press, crowded.

He toke hys sweard and hys buckler,

And among them all he ran,

Where the people were most in prece

He smote downe many a man.

37.

There myght no man stand hys stroke,

So fersly on them he ran:

Then they threw wyndowes and dores on him

And so toke that good yeman.

38.

There they hym bounde both hand and fote,

And in a deepe dongeon him cast:

'Now, Cloudesle,' sayd the hye justice,

'Thou shalt be hanged in hast.'

39.

'One vow shal I make,' sayde the sherife,

'A payre of new gallowes shal I for thee make;

And all the gates of Carlile shal be shutte:
There shall no man come in therat.
40.
'Then shall not helpe Clym of the Cloughe,
Nor yet Adam Bell,
Though they came with a thousand mo,
Nor all the devels in hell.'
41.
Early in the mornyng the justice uprose,
To the gates fast gan he gon,
And commaunded to be shut full close
Lightile everychone.

42.
Then went he to the markett place,
As fast as he coulde hye;
A payre of new gallowes there dyd he up set,
Besyde the pyllorye.
43.
A lytle boy stood them among,
And asked what meaned that gallow-tre?
They sayde, 'To hange a good yeman,
Called Wyllyam of Cloudesle.'
44.
That lytle boye was the towne swyne-heard,
And kept fayre Alyce swyne;
Full oft he had seene Cloudesle in the wodde,
And geven hym there to dyne.
45.

45.³ 'wight,' active.

He went out of a crevis in the wall,

And lightly to the woode dyd gone;

There met he with these wight yonge men

Shortly and anone.

46.

'Alas!' then sayde that lytle boye,

'Ye tary here all too longe;

Cloudeslee is taken, and dampned to death,

All readye for to honge.'

47.

'Alas!' then sayd good Adam Bell,

'That ever we see thys daye!

He might here with us have dwelled,

So ofte as we dyd him praye.

48.

48.⁴ 'teene,' sorrow.

'He myght have taryed in grene foreste,

Under the shadowes sheene,

And have kepte both hym and us in reste,

Out of trouble and teene.'

49.

Adam bent a ryght good bow,

A great hart sone had he slayne:

'Take that, chylde,' he sayde, 'to thy dynner,

And bryng me myne arrowe agayne.'

50.

50.³ 'borowe,' redeem, liberate.

'Now go we hence,' sayed these wight yong men,
'Tarry we no longer here;
We shall hym borowe, by God's grace,
Though we buy itt full dere.'

51.
To Caerlel wente these good yemen,
In a mery mornyng of Maye.
Here is a fyt of Cloudesly,
And another is for to saye.

52.
And when they came to mery Caerlell,
In a fayre mornyng-tyde,
They founde the gates shut them untyll
Round about on every syde.

53.
'Alas!' than sayd good Adam Bell,
'That ever we were made men!
These gates be shut so wonderly well,
That we may not come herein.'

54.
Than spake Clym of the Clough,
'Wyth a wyle we wyl us in bryng;
Let us saye we be messengers,
Streyght comen from our king.'

55.
Adam said, 'I have a letter written wele,
Now let us wysely werke,
We wyl saye we have the kyngës seale;

I holde the porter no clerke.'

56.

56.[4] 'thronge,' pressed, hastened.

Than Adam Bell bete on the gate

With strokës great and stronge:

The porter herde suche a noyse therat,

And to the gate faste he thronge.

57.

'Who is there now,' sayde the porter,

'That maketh all this knockinge?'

'We be two messengers,' sayd Clim of the Clough,

'Be comen streyght from our kyng.'

58.

'We have a letter,' sayd Adam Bell,

'To the justice we must it bryng;

Let us in our message to do,

That we were agayne to our kyng.'

59.

'Here commeth no man in,' sayd the porter,

'By hym that dyed on a tre,

Tyll a false thefe be hanged

Called Wyllyam of Cloudesle.'

60.

Than spake that good yeman Clym of the Clough,

And swore by Mary fre,

'If that we stande long wythout,

Lyke a thefe hanged shalt thou be.

61.

61.² 'lordane,' sluggard: 'wode,' mad.
'Lo! here we have got the kyngës seale:
What, lordane, art thou wode?'
The porter had wende it had ben so,
And lyghtly dyd off hys hode.
62.
'Welcome be my lordes seale,' saide he;
'For that ye shall come in.'
He opened the gate right shortly:
An evyl openyng for him!
63.
'Now we are in,' sayde Adam Bell,
'Therof we are full faine;
But Christ knoweth, that harowed hell,
How we shall com out agayne.'
64.
'Had we the keys,' said Clim of the Clough,
'Ryght wel than shoulde we spede,
Than might we come out wel ynough
Whan we se tyme and nede.'

65.
They called the porter to a councell,
And wrong his necke in two,
And caste hym in a depe dongeon,
And toke the keys hym fro.
66.
'Now am I porter,' sayd Adam Bel,
'Se, brother, the keys have we here,

The worst porter to mery Carlile
That ye had thys hondreth yere.

67.

'Now wyll we our bowës bend,
Into the towne wyll we go,
For to delyver our dere brother,
Where he lyeth in care and wo.'

68.

68.⁴ 'stound,' time.

Then they bent theyr good yew bowes,
And loked theyr stringes were round;
The markett place of mery Carlile
They beset in that stound.

69.

69.³ 'squyers': an earlier text gives 'swerers.'

And, as they loked them besyde,
A paire of new galowes there they see,
And the justice with a quest of squyers,
That judged William hanged to be.

70.

And Cloudesle hymselfe lay ready in a cart
Fast bound both fote and hand;
And a stronge rope about hys necke,
All readye for to be hangde.

71.

The justice called to him a ladde,
Cloudesles clothes shold he have,
To take the measure of that good yoman,

And thereafter to make hys grave.

72.

72.² 'pryme'; see 9.³, note.

'I have sene as great a mervaile,' said Cloudesle,

'As betweyne thys and pryme,

He that maketh thys grave for me,

Hymselfe may lye therin.'

73.

'Thou speakest proudlye,' said the justice,

'I shall hange thee with my hande.'

Full wel that herd his brethren two

There styl as they dyd stande.

74.

Then Cloudesle cast his eyen asyde,

And saw hys brethren stande

At a corner of the market place,

With theyr good bowes bent in theyr hand,

Redy the justyce for to chase.

75.

'I se good comfort,' sayd Cloudesle,

'Yet hope I well to fare,

If I might have my handes at wyll

Ryght lytel wold I care.'

76.

Than bespake good Adam Bell

To Clym of the Clough so free,

'Brother, se ye marke the justyce wel;

Lo! yonder ye may him se:

77.

'And at the shyrife shote I wyll

Strongly wyth an arrowe kene;

A better shote in mery Carlile

Thys seven yere was not sene.'

78.

They loosed their arrowes both at once,

Of no man had they drede;

The one hyt the justice, the other the sheryfe,

That both theyr sides gan blede.

79.

All men voyded, that them stode nye,

Whan the justice fell to the grounde,

And the sherife fell nye hym by;

Eyther had his deathës wounde.

80.

All the citezens fast gan fle,

They durst no longer abyde:

There lyghtly they loosed Cloudeslee,

Where he with ropes lay tyde.

81.

Wyllyam stert to an officer of the towne,

Hys axe out hys hand he wronge,

On eche syde he smote them downe,

Hym thought he had taryed too long.

82.

Wyllyam sayde to hys brethren two,

'Thys daye let us lyve and die,

If ever you have nede, as I have now,

The same shall you finde by me.'

83.

They shot so well in that tyde,

For theyr stringes were of silke ful sure,

That they kept the stretes on every side;

That batayle did long endure.

84.

They fought together as brethren true,

Lyke hardy men and bolde,

Many a man to the ground they threw,

And made many an hertë colde.

85.

But whan their arrowes were all gon,

Men presyd on them full fast,

They drew theyr swordës than anone,

And theyr bowës from them cast.

86.

They went lyghtlye on theyr way,

Wyth swordes and buclers round;

By that it was the myddes of the day,

They had made many a wound.

87.

87.[1] Horns blown to call the citizens to support the civil authorities.

There was many an out-horne in Carleil blowen,

And the belles backward dyd they ryng,

Many a woman sayde 'Alas!'

And many theyr handes dyd wryng.

88.

The mayre of Carlile forth com was,
And wyth hym a full great route:
These three yemen dred hym full sore,
For theyr lyvës stode in doute.

89.

89.⁴ 'stoure,' fight, disturbance.

The mayre came armed, a full great pace,
With a polaxe in hys hande;
Many a strong man wyth him was,
There in that stoure to stande.

90.

The mayre smote at Cloudesle with his bil,
Hys bucler he brast in two,
Full many a yoman with great yll,
'Alas! Treason,' they cryed for wo.
'Kepe we the gates fast,' they bad,
'That these traytours therout not go.'

91.

91.⁴ 'at a braide,' in a moment.

But al for nought was that they wrought,
For so fast they downe were layde,
Tyll they all thre, that so manfully fought,
Were gotten without at a braide.

92.

'Have here your keys,' sayd Adam Bel,
'Myne office I here forsake,
Yf you do by my councell
A newë porter ye make.'

93.

93.³ 'letteth,' hinders.

He threw the keys there at theyr heads,
And bad them evil to thryve,
And all that letteth any good yoman
To come and comfort his wyfe.

94.

94.³ 'lynde,' tree: cp. 101.². Here perhaps it means linden.

Thus be these good yomen gon to the wode,
As lyghtly as lefe on lynde;
They laugh and be mery in theyr mode,
Theyr enemyes were farr behynde.

95.

Whan they came to Inglyswode,
Under their trysty-tre,
There they found bowës full good,
And arrowës great plentë.

96.

96.⁴ 'meynë,' troop, company.

'So help me God,' sayd Adam Bell,
And Clym of the Clough so fre,
'I would we were nowe in mery Carlile,
Before that fayre meynë.'

97.

They set them downe, and made good chere,
And eate and dranke full well.
Here is a fytte of the wight yongemen:
And another I shall you tell.

98.

As they sat in Inglyswood,

Under theyr trysty-tre,

They thought they herd a woman wepe,

But her they myght not se.

99.

Sore syghed there fayre Alyce, and sayd,

'Alas, that ever I see thys day!

For nowe is my dere husband slayne:

Alas! and wel-a-way!

100.

'Myght I have spoken wyth hys dere brethren,

With eyther of them twayne,

To show to them what him befell,

My hart were out of payne.'

101.

Cloudesle walked a lytle beside,

And looked under the grene wood lynde,

He was ware of his wife and chyldren three,

Full wo in herte and mynde.

102.

'Welcome, wyfe,' than sayde Wyllyam,

'Unto this trysty-tre:

I had wende yesterday, by swete saynt John,

Thou sholde me never have se.'

103.

'Now well is me,' she sayd, 'that ye be here,

My harte is out of wo.'

'Dame,' he sayde, 'be mery and glad,

And thanke my brethren two.'

104.

104.² 'no bote,' no boot, *i.e.* no advantage.

'Herof to speake,' said Adam Bell,

'I-wis it is no bote:

The meate, that we must supp withall,

It runneth yet fast on fote.'

105.

105.¹ 'launde,' lawn, glade, clearing.

105.³ 'a hart of grece,' a fat hart (Fr. graisse).

Then went they downe into a launde,

These noble archares all thre;

Eche of them slew a hart of grece,

The best they cold there se.

106.

'Have here the best, Alyce my wyfe,'

Sayde Wyllyam of Cloudeslye,

'By cause ye so boldly stode me by

Whan I was slayne full nye.'

107.

Than went they to theyr suppere

Wyth suche meate as they had;

And thanked God of ther fortune:

They were both mery and glad.

108.

108.² 'lease,' falsehood. Cp. 115.², 132.², 134.³, *et passim*.

And when they had supped well,

Certayne withouten lease,

Cloudesle sayd, 'We wyll to our kyng,

To get us a charter of peace.

109.

'Alyce shal be at sojournyng

In a nunnery here besyde;

My two sonnes shall wyth her go,

And there they shall abyde.

110.

'Myne eldest son shall go wyth me;

For hym have I no care:

And he shall bring you worde agayn,

How that we do fare.'

111.

Thus be these wight men to London gone,

As fast as they maye hye,

Tyll they came to the kynges pallace;

There they woulde nedës be.

112.

And whan they came to the kyngës courte,

Unto the pallace gate,

Of no man wold they aske leave,

But boldly went in therat.

113.

113.[1] 'presily,' promptly.

They presyd prestly into the hall,

Of no man had they dreade:

The porter came after, and dyd them calle,

And with them began to chyde.
114.

114.³ 'shent,' scolded, blamed.

The usher sayde, 'Yemen, what wold ye have?
I pray you tell to me:
You myght thus make offycers shent:
Good syrs, of whence be ye?'
115.

'Syr, we be outlawes of the forest
Certayne withouten lease;
And hyther we be come to our kyng,
To get us a charter of peace.'
116.

And whan they came before the kyng,
As it was the lawe of the lande,
They kneled downe without lettyng,
And eche held up his hand.

117.

They sayed, 'Lord, we beseche you here,
That ye wyll graunt us grace;
For we have slayne your fat falow dere
In many a sondry place.'
118.

'What is your names,' than said our king,
'Anone that you tell me?'
They sayd, 'Adam Bell, Clim of the Clough,
And Wyllyam of Cloudesle.'
119.

'Be ye those theves,' than sayd our kyng,
'That men have tolde of to me?
Here to God I make a vowe,
Ye shal be hanged al thre.

120.
'Ye shal be dead without mercy,
As I am kynge of this lande.'
He commanded his officers everichone,
Fast on them to lay hande.

121.
There they toke these good yemen,
And arested them al thre:
'So may I thryve,' sayd Adam Bell,
'Thys game lyketh not me.

122.
'But, good lorde, we beseche you now,
That ye wyll graunt us grace,
Insomuche as we be to you comen,
Or elles that we may fro you passe,

123.
'With such weapons, as we have here,
Tyll we be out of your place;
And yf we lyve this hondred yere,
We wyll aske you no grace.'

124.
'Ye speake proudly,' sayd the kynge;
'Ye shall be hanged all thre.'
'That were great pitye,' sayd the quene,

'If any grace myght be.

125.

125.⁴ 'belyfe,' immediately. The word is spelled in many ways.

'My lorde, whan I came fyrst into this lande

To be your wedded wyfe,

The fyrst boone that I would aske,

Ye would graunt me belyfe:

126.

'And I asked you never none tyll now;

Therefore, good lorde, graunt it me.'

'Now aske it, madam,' sayd the kynge,

'And graunted shal it be.'

127.

'Than, good lord, I you beseche,

These yemen graunt you me.'

'Madame, ye myght have asked a boone,

That shuld have been worth them thre.

128.

128.³ 'pay,' satisfaction.

'Ye myght have asked towres, and townes,

Parkes and forestes plentie.'

'None soe pleasant to my pay,' shee sayd;

'Nor none so lefe to me.'

129.

'Madame, sith it is your desyre,

Your askyng graunted shal be;

But I had lever have given you

Good market townës thre.'

130.

The quene was a glad woman,

And sayde, 'Lord, gramarcy;

I dare undertake for them,

That true men shal they be.

131.

'But, good lord, speke som mery word,

That comfort they may se.'

'I graunt you grace,' than sayd our kyng;

'Washe, felos, and to meate go ye.'

132.

They had not setten but a whyle

Certayne without lesynge,

There came messengers out of the north

With letters to our kyng.

133.

And whan they came before the kynge,

They kneled downe upon theyr kne;

And sayd, 'Lord, your officers grete you well,

Of Carlile in the north cuntre.'

134.

'How fareth my justice,' sayd the kyng,

'And my sherife also?'

'Syr, they be slayne, without lesynge,

And many an officer mo.'

135.

'Who hath them slayne?' sayd the kyng;

'Anone thou tell me.'

'Adam Bell, and Clim of the Clough,

And Wyllyam of Cloudesle.'

136.

136.¹ 'rewth,' pity.

'Alas for rewth!' than said our kynge:

'My hart is wonderous sore;

I had lever than a thousande pounde,

I had knowne of thys before;

137.

137.² 'forthynketh me,' seems serious to me, troubles me.

'For I have y-graunted them grace,

And that forthynketh me:

But had I knowne all thys before,

They had been hanged all thre.'

138.

The kyng opened the letter anone,

Himselfe he red it tho,

And founde how these thre outlawes had slain

Thre hundred men and mo:

139.

139.³ 'catchipolles,' sheriff's officers.

Fyrst the justice, and the sheryfe,

And the mayre of Carlile towne;

Of all the constables and catchipolles

Alyve were left not one:

140.

140.³ 'fosters of the fe,' —'a person who had for some service to the crown a perpetual right of hunting in a forest on paying to the crown a certain rent for the same.' —HALLIWELL.

The baylyes, and the bedyls both,

And the sergeauntes of the law,

And forty fosters of the fe,

These outlawes had y-slaw:

141.

And broke his parks, and slayne his dere;

Over all they chose the best;

So perelous out-lawes as they were

Walked not by easte nor west.

142.

When the kynge this letter had red,

In hys harte he syghed sore:

'Take up the table,' anone he bad,

'For I may eat no more.'

143.

The kyng called his best archars

To the buttes wyth hym to go:

'I wyll se these felowes shote,' he sayd,

'That in the north have wrought this wo.'

144.

144.[1] prepared themselves instantly.

The kynges bowmen buske them blyve.

And the quenes archers also;

So dyd these thre wyght yemen;

With them they thought to go.

145.

There twyse or thryse they shote about

For to assay theyr hande;

There was no shote these thre yemen shot.

That any prycke myght them stand.

146.

Then spake Wyllyam of Cloudesle;

'By God that for me dyed,

I hold hym never no good archar,

That shoteth at buttes so wyde.'

147.

'Whereat?' than sayd our king,

'I pray thee tell me.'

'At suche a but, syr,' he sayd.

'As men use in my countree.'

148.

Wyllyam wente into a fyeld,

And his two brethren with him:

There they set up two hasell roddes

Twenty score paces betwene.

149.

'I hold him an archar,' said Cloudesle,

'That yonder wande cleveth in two.'

'Here is none suche,' sayd the kyng,

'Nor none that can so do.'

150.

150.[3] 'bearyng arowe,' ? a very long arrow, such as requires to be carried in the hand. Cf. *Sir Andrew Barton*, 53.[3].

'I shall assaye, syr,' sayd Cloudesle,

'Or that I farther go.'

Cloudesly with a bearyng arowe

Clave the wand in two.

151.

'Thou art the best archer,' then said the king,

'Forsothe that ever I se.'

'And yet for your love,' sayd Wyllyam,

'I wyll do more maystry.

152.

'I have a sonne is seven yere olde,

He is to me full deare;

I wyll hym tye to a stake;

All shall se, that be here;

153.

'And lay an apple upon hys head,

And go syxe score paces hym fro,

And I my selfe with a brode arow

Shall cleve the apple in two.'

154.

'Now haste thee then sayd the kyng,

'By hym that dyed on a tre;

But yf thou do not as thou hest sayde,

Hanged shalt thou be.

155.

155.[1] 'And,' if.

'And thou touche his head or gowne,

In syght that men may se,

By all the sayntes that be in heaven,

I shall hange you all thre.'

156.

'That I have promised,' said William,

'I wyll it never forsake.'

And there even before the kynge
In the earth he drove a stake:
157.
And bound therto his eldest sonne,
And bad hym stand styll thereat;
And turned the childes face fro him,
Because he should not stert.
158.
158.³ 'outmet,' measured out.
An apple upon his head he set,
And then his bowe he bent:
Syxe score paces they were outmet,
And thether Cloudesle went.
159.
There he drew out fayre brode arrowe,
Hys bowe was great and longe,
He set that arrowe in his bowe,
That was both styffe and stronge.

160.
He prayed the people, that wer there,
That they wold still stand,
For he that shoteth for such a wager
Behoveth a stedfast hand.
161.
Muche people prayed for Cloudesle,
That his lyfe saved myght be,
And whan he made hym redy to shote,
There was many a weeping eye.

162.

Thus Cloudesle clefte the apple in two,

That many a man it se:

'Over Gods forbode,' sayde the kinge,

'That thou sholdest shote at me.

163.

'I geve thee eightene pence a day,

And my bowe shalt thou bere,

And over all the north countre

I make the chyfe rydere.'

164.

'And I give thee twelve pence a day,' said the quene,

'By God and by my fay;

Come feche thy payment whan thou wylt,

No man shall say thee nay.'

165.

165.[2] 'fe,' money.

'Wyllyam, I make thee gentleman

Of clothyng and of fe:

And thy two brethren yemen of my chambre,

For they are so semely to see.

166.

'Your sonne, for he is tendre of age,

Of my wyne-seller shall he be;

And whan he commeth to mannës state,

Better avaunced shall he be.'

167.

'And, Wyllyam, bring me your wife,' said the quene,

'Me longeth sore her to see:

She shall be my chefe gentlewoman,

And governe my nursery.'

168.

The yemen thanked them full curteously;

And sayd, 'To Rome streyght wyll we wend,

Of all the synnes that we have done

To be assoyled of his hand.'

169.

So forth be gone these good yemen,

As fast as they might hye;

And after came and dwelled with the kynge,

And dyed good men all thre.

170.

Thus endeth the lives of these good yemen;

God send them eternall blysse,

And all that with hand-bowe shoteth,

That of heven they may never mysse!

JOHNNY O' COCKLEY'S WELL

THE TEXT is taken almost entirely from a copy which was sent in 1780 to Bishop Percy by a Miss Fisher of Carlisle; in the last half of the first stanza her version gives, unintelligibly:

> 'But little knew he that his bloody hounds
>
> Were bound in iron bands':

and I have therefore substituted lines from a later text. The correction in 20.[1] and 21.[1] is also essential.

THE STORY will be familiar to many as *Johnie of Breadislee*, a title given by Sir Walter Scott to his version, the first that was published, in the *Minstrelsy* (1802). In the present version, however, Johnny certainly belongs to Cockley's Well, Bradyslee being only the name of his hunting-ground. In other variants, his name is Johnny Cock, Johnny Cox, Johnny o' Cockis, o' Cockerslee, of Cockielaw, of Cocklesmuir, or Johnny Brad. The name of the hunting-ground varies also, though not so widely; and, as usual, the several editors of the ballad have carefully noted that its topography (though the nomenclature is corrupted) connects it with this district or that—Percy's ballad is Northumbrian, Scott's is of Dumfriesshire.

Percy considered that the mention of wolves (17.[1]) was an indication of the antiquity of the ballad; whereupon Child quotes Holinshed (1577) as saying that 'though the island is void of wolves south of the Tweed, yet the Scots cannot boast the like, since they have grievous wolves.' Yet how can one reconcile the mention of wolves with the reference to 'American leather' (13.[3])?

Professor Child calls this a 'precious specimen of the unspoiled traditional ballad,' and Professor Gummere points out that 'it goes with a burden, this sterling old song, and has traces of an incremental repetition that has been reduced to lowest terms by impatient transcribers' (*The Popular Ballad*, p. 268). In his *Old English Ballads* Gummere gives a text very ingeniously compounded of Percy's and Kinloch's; and Professor Brandl has attempted to restore the original text.

JOHNNY O' COCKLEY'S WELL

1.

1.[2-5] From Kinloch's version. The final repetition, here printed in italics, forms the burden in singing, and is to be repeated, *mutatis mutandis*, in each verse.

JOHNNY he has risen up i' the morn,
Call'd for water to wash his hands;
And he has called for his good grey-hounds
That lay bound in iron bands, *bands,*
That lay bound in iron bands.
2.
2.[2] 'care-bed,' the bed of sickness due to anxiety.
Johnny's mother has gotten word o' that,
And care-bed she has taen.
'O Johnny, for my benison,
I beg you'll stay at hame;
For the wine so red, and the well-baken bread,
My Johnny shall want nane.

3.
3.[1] 'forsters,' foresters, woodmen.
'There are seven forsters at Pickeram Side,
At Pickeram where they dwell,
And for a drop of thy heart's bluid
They wad ride the fords of hell.'
4.
Johnny he's gotten word of that,
And he's turned wondrous keen;
He's put off the red scarlet,
And he's put on the Lincoln green.
5.
With a sheaf of arrows by his side,
And a bent bow in his hand,
He's mounted on a prancing steed,

And he has ridden fast o'er the strand.

6.

6.¹ The MS. reads 'Braidhouplee' for the first 'Bradyslee.'

6.² 'buss,' bush.

He's up i' Bradyslee, and down i' Bradyslee,
And under a buss o' broom;
And there he found a good dun deer
Feeding in a buss of ling.

7.

7.⁴ 'stem'd,' stopped, stayed.

7.¹ 'lap,' leapt.

Johnny shot, and the dun deer lap,
And she lap wondrous wide,
Until they came to the wan water,
And he stem'd her of her pride.

8.

8.⁴ 'but and,' and.

He has taen out the little pen-knife,
'Twas full three quarters long,
And he has taen out of that dun deer
The liver but and the tongue.

9.

They eat of the flesh, and they drank of the blood,
And the blood it was so sweet,
Which caused Johnny and his bloody hounds
To fall in a deep sleep.

10.

10.⁴ 'drie,' hold out, be able.

By then came an old palmer,

And an ill death may he die!

For he's away to Pickeram Side,

As fast as he can drie.

11.

'What news, what news?' says the Seven Forsters,

'What news have ye brought to me?'

'I have no news,' the palmer said,

'But what I saw with my eye.

12.

12.² 'scroggs,' underwood.

12.³ 'well-wight,' stalwart.

'High up i' Bradyslee, low down i' Bradyslee,

And under a buss of scroggs,

O there I spied a well-wight man

Sleeping among his dogs.

13.

13.³ 'American leather.' A patent for making morocco from American horsehides was granted c. 1799, but the date of this text is twenty years earlier than that date.

'His coat it was of the light Lincoln,

And his breeches of the same,

His shoes of the American leather,

And gold buckles tying them.'

14.

Up bespake the Seven Forsters,

Up bespake they ane and a':

'O that is Johnny o' Cockley's Well,

And near him we will draw.'

15.

15.[1] 'ae' (y in the MS.), one. Cf. 21.[3].

O the first ae stroke that they gae him,

They struck him off by the knee;

Then up bespake his sister's son:

'O the next'll gar him die!'

16.

'O some they count ye well-wight men,

But I do count ye nane;

For you might well ha' waken'd me,

And ask'd gin I wad be taen.

17.

'The wildest wolf in a' this wood

Wad not ha' done so by me;

She'd ha' wet her foot i' th' wan water,

And sprinkled it o'er my bree,

And if that wad not ha' waken'd me,

She wad ha' gone and let me be.

18.

18.[3] 'belive,' quickly.

'O bows of yew, if ye be true,

In London, where ye were bought,

Fingers five, get up belive,

Manhuid shall fail me nought.'

19.

19.[3] 'wan,' won, reached.

19.[4] The MS. gives 'bord (or bood) words.'

He has kill'd the Seven Forsters,

He has kill'd them all but ane,

And that wan scarce to Pickeram Side,
To carry the bode-words hame.

20.
20.[1], 21.[1]: The MS. gives 'boy' for 'bird.'
'Is there never a bird in a' this wood
That will tell what I can say;
That will go to Cockley's Well,
Tell my mither to fetch me away?'
21.
There was a bird into that wood,
That carried the tidings away,
And many ae was the well-wight man
At the fetching o' Johnny away.

THE OUTLAW MURRAY

THE TEXT is derived, with trivial alterations, from Herd's MSS. In the first edition of the *Minstrelsy of the Scottish Border*, Scott says the principal copy he employed was one 'apparently of considerable antiquity' among the papers of Mrs. Cockburn; he also made use of Herd's MS. and the Glenriddell MS. In the second edition of the *Minstrelsy* he made further additions, including one of three stanzas between 52 and 58 of the present version, which makes reference to an earlier Sir Walter Scott.

THE STORY of this Scots outlaw makes tame reading after those which precede it in this volume. The ballad was inserted at the end of Child's collection only because he preferred 'to err by including rather than excluding.' He adds, 'I am convinced that it did not begin its existence as a popular ballad, and I am not convinced that (as Scott asserts) it has been for ages a popular song in Selkirkshire.' Nevertheless, it undoubtedly gained a place in popular tradition; and this, while entitling it to a place here, renders the elaborate historical investigation, to which it has been submitted since Child's edition, a waste of erudition and ingenuity.

THE OUTLAW MURRAY

1.

ETTRICK Forest is a fair forest,

In it grows many a seemly tree;

The hart, the hynd, the doe, the roe,

And of a' wild beastis great plentie.

2.

2.[1] 'biggit,' built.

There's a castell biggit with lime and stane;

O gin it stands not pleasantlie!

In the forefront o' that castell fair,

Twa unicorns are bra' to see.

3.

There's the picture of a knight, and a ladye bright,

And the grene hollin abune their bree;
There an Outlaw keeps five hundred men;
He keeps a royal companie.
4.
His merry men are in ae liverie clad,
Of the Lincoln grene sae fair to see;
He and his ladie in purple clad,
O gin they live not royallie!
5.
5.4 'courtrie,' courtiers.
Word is gane to our noble king,
In Edinburgh, where that he lay,
That there was an Outlaw in Ettrick Forest
Counted him nought and all his courtrie gay.
6.
'I mak a vow,' then the gude king said,
'Unto the man that dear bought me,
I'se either be king of Ettrick Forest
Or king of Scotland that Outlaw's be.'
7.
Then spak the earl hight Hamilton,
And to the noble king said he,
'My sovereign prince, some counsel take,
First of your nobles, syne of me.

8.
8.1 'redd,' advise.
'I redd ye, send yon bra' Outlaw till,
And see gif your man come will he:

Desire him come and be your man,

And hold of you yon forest free.

9.

'And gif he refuses to do that,

We'll conquer both his lands and he,

Or else we'll throw his castell down,

And mak a widow o' his gay ladye.'

10.

The king called on a gentleman,

James Boyd, Earl of Arran, his brother was he;

When James he came before the king,

He fell before him on his knee.

11.

'Welcome, James Boyd,' said our noble king;

'A message ye maun gang for me;

Ye maun hie to Ettrick Forest,

To yon Outlaw, where dwelleth he;

12.

'Ask him of whom he holds his lands,

Or, man, who may his master be,

Desire him come and be my man,

And hold of me yon forest free.

13.

'To Edinburgh to come and gang,

His safe-warrant I sall be;

And gif he refuses to do that,

We'll conquer baith his lands and he.

14.

14.[4] 'frith,' wood.

'Thou may'st vow I'll cast his castell down,
And mak a widow o' his gay ladye;
I'll hang his merry men pair by pair
In ony frith where I may them see.'

15.

James Boyd took his leave of the noble king,
To Ettrick Forest fair cam he;
Down Birkendale Brae when that he cam,
He saw the fair forest with his ee.

16.

16.[4] 'whidderand,' whizzing.

Baith doe and roe and hart and hind
And of a' wild beastis great plentie;
He heard the bows that bauldly ring,
And arrows whidderand near him by.

17.

Of that fair castell he got a sight;
The like he nere saw with his ee;
On the forefront o' that castell
Twa unicorns were bra' to see.

18.

The picture of a knight, and a lady bright,
And the green hollin abune their bree;
Thereat he spy'd five hundred men,
Shooting with bows upon the lee.

19.

They a' were in ae livery clad,
O' the Lincoln green sae fair to see;

The knight and his ladye in purple clad;
O gif they lived right royallie!
Therefore he kend he was master-man,
And served him in his ain degree.

20.
'God mot thee save, brave Outlaw Murray,
Thy ladye and a' thy chivalrie!'
'Marry, thou's welcome, gentleman,
Some king's-messenger thou seems to be.'
21.
'The King of Scotland sent me here,
And, gude Outlaw, I'm sent to thee;
I wad wot of whom ye hold your lands,
Or, man, wha may thy master be?'
22.
22.³ 'Soudron,' Southron, *i.e.* southern, English.
'Thir landis are mine,' the Outlaw said;
'I own na king in Christentie;
Frae Soudron I this forest wan,
Whan the king nor 's knights were not to see.'
23.
'He desires you'll come to Edinburgh,
And hold of him this forest free;
And gif you refuse to do this,
He'll conquer baith thy landis and thee;
He has vow'd to cast thy castell down,
And mak a widow o' thy gay ladye;
24.

'He'll hang thy merry men pair by pair
In ony frith where he may them find.'
'Aye, by my troth!' the Outlaw said,
'Than wad I think me far behind.
25.
'Ere the king my fair countrie get,
This land that 's nativest to me,
Mony o' his nobles sall be cauld,
Their ladyes sall be right wearie.'

26.
26.⁴ 'rad,' afraid.
Then spak his ladye, fair of face,
She said, 'Without consent of me,
That an Outlaw shuld come before the king;
I am right rad of treasonrie.
27.
'Bid him be gude to his lordis at hame,
For Edinburgh my lord sail never see.'
James tuke his leave of the Outlaw keen,
To Edinburgh boun is he.
28.
And when he cam before the king,
He fell before him on his knee:
'Welcome, James Boyd!' said the noble king;
'What forest is Ettrick Forest free?'
29.
'Ettrick Forest is the fairest forest
That ever man saw with his ee;

There's the doe, the roe, the hart, the hynde,
And of a' wild beastis great plentie.

30.

'There's a pretty castell of lime and stane,
O gif it stands not pleasauntlie!
There's on the foreside of that castell
Twa unicorns sae bra' to see.

31.

'There's the picture of a knight, and a ladye bright,
And the green hollin abune their bree.
There the Outlaw keepis five hundred men,
O gif they live not royallie!

32.

'His merry men in ae livery clad,
O' the Lincoln green so fair to see;
He and his ladye in purple clad;
O! gif they live not royallie!

33.

'He says yon forest is his ain,
He wan it from the Soudronie;
Sae as he wan it, sae will he keep it,
Contrair all kings in Christentie.'

34.

34.[1] 'Gar ray,' cause to be arrayed, *i.e.* saddled.
34.[3] 'graith,' equip, prepare.

'Gar ray my horse,' said the noble king,
'To Ettrick Forest hie will I me';
Then he gard graith five thousand men,

And sent them on for the forest free.
35.
Then word is gane the Outlaw till,
In Ettrick Forest, where dwelleth he,
That the king was coming to his cuntrie,
To conquer baith his lands and he.
36.
'I mak a vow,' the Outlaw said,
'I mak a vow, and that trulie,
Were there but three men to take my part
Yon king's coming full dear suld be.'
37.
Then messengers he called forth,
And bade them haste them speedilie:
'Ane of you go to Halliday,
The laird of the Covehead is he.

38.
'He certain is my sister's son;
Bid him come quick and succour me;
Tell Halliday with thee to come,
And show him a' the veritie.'
39.
'What news, what news?' said Halliday,
'Man, frae thy master unto me?'
'Not as ye wad; seeking your aid;
The king's his mortal enemie.'
40.
'Aye, by my troth,' quoth Halliday,

'Even for that it repenteth me;
For gif he lose fair Ettrick Forest,
He'll tak fair Moffatdale frae me.

41.

41.² 'mae,' more.

'I'll meet him wi' five hundred men,
And surely mae, if mae may be.'
The Outlaw call'd a messenger,
And bid him hie him speedily.

42.

'To Andrew Murray of Cockpool,
That man's a dear cousin to me;
Desire him come, and make me aid,
With all the power that he may be.

43.

'The king has vow'd to cast my castle down,
And mak a widow of my gay ladye;
He'll hang my merry men pair by pair
In ony place where he may them see.'

44.

'It stands me hard,' quoth Andrew Murray,
'Judge if it stands not hard with me;
To enter against a king with crown,
And put my lands in jeopardie!

45.

'Yet gif I come not on the day,
Surely at night he sall me see.'
To Sir James Murray, laird of Traquair,

A message came right speedilie.

46.

'What news, what news?' James Murray said,

'Man, frae thy master unto me?'

'What need I tell? for wel ye ken

The king's his mortal enemie.

47.

'He desires ye'll come and make him aid,

With all the powers that ye may be.'

'And, by my troth,' James Murray said,

'With that Outlaw will I live and die;

48.

'The king has gifted my lands lang syne,

It can not be nae war with me.'

. . . . .
. . . . .

49.

49.[1] A ford on the Tweed, at the mouth of the Caddon Burn, near Yair.

The king was coming thro' Caddon Ford,

And fifteen thousand men was he;

They saw the forest them before,

They thought it awsome for to see.

50.

Then spak the earl hight Hamilton,

And to the noble king said he,

'My sovereign prince, some counsel take,

First at your nobles, syne at me.

51.

'Desire him meet thee at Penman's Core,

And bring four in his companie;

Five earls sall gang yoursell before,

Gude cause that you suld honour'd be.

52.

'And, if he refuses to do that,

Wi' fire and sword we'll follow thee;

There sall never a Murray, after him,

Have land in Ettrick Forest free.'

53.

The king then call'd a gentleman,

Royal banner-bearer then was he;

James Hope Pringle of Torsonse, by name:

He came and knelit upon his knee.

54.

'Welcome, James Pringle of Torsonse!

Ye maun a message gae for me;

Ye maun gae to yon Outlaw Murray,

Surely where bauldly bideth he.

55.

'Bid him meet me at Penman's Core,

And bring four of his companie;

Five earls sall come wi' mysel,

Gude reason I suld honour'd be.

56.

'And if he refuses to do that,

Bid him look for nae good o' me;

There sall never a Murray after him

Have land in Ettrick Forest free.'

57.

James came before the Outlaw keen,
And served him in his ain degree;
'Welcome, James Pringle of Torsonse!
What tidings frae the king to me?'

58.

'He bids you meet him at Penman's Core,
And bring four of your companie;
Five earls will come with the king,
Mae mair in number will he be.

59.

'And gif you refuse to do that,
I freely here upgive wi' thee,
There will never a Murray after thee
Have land in Ettrick Forest free.

60.

'He'll cast your bonny castle down,
And make a widow of your gaye ladye,
He'll hang your merry men pair by pair
In ony place where he may them see.'

61.

'It stands me hard,' the Outlaw said;
'Judge if it stands not hard with me;
I reck not of losing of mysell,
But all my offspring after me.

62.

'Auld Halliday, young Halliday,
Ye sall be twa to gang wi' me;

Andrew Murray, and Sir James Murray,

We'll be nae mae in companie.'

63.

When that they came before the king,

They fell befor him on their knee;

'Grant mercy, mercy, royal king!

E'en for His sake who died on tree.'

64.

64.[1] 'Siccan,' such.

'Siecan like mercie sall ye have;

On gallows ye sall hangit be!'

'God forbid,' quo' the Outlaw then,

'I hope your grace will better be!'

65.

'These lands of Ettrick Forest fair,

I wan them frae the enemie;

Like as I wan them, sae will I keep them,

Contrair all kings in Christentie.'

66.

All the nobles said, the king about,

Pitie it were to see him die:

'Yet grant me mercy, sovereign prince,

Extend your favour unto me!

67.

'I'll give you the keys of my castell,

With the blessing o' my fair ladye,

Mak me the sheriff of the forest,

And all my offspring after me.'

68.

'Wilt thou give me the keys of thy castell,

With the blessing of thy fair ladye?

I'll mak thee sheriff of the Forest,

Surely while upwards grows the tree;

If you be not traitour to the king,

Forfaulted sall ye never be.'

69.

'But, prince, what sall come o' my men?

When I go back, traitour they'll ca' me.

I had rather lose my life and land,

Ere my merry men rebukëd me.'

70.

'Will your merry men amend their lives?

And all their pardons I grant thee;

Now, name thy landes where'er they be,

And here I render them to thee.'

71.

71.[4] 'steads,' dwelling-places. Cp. farm-stead, home-stead.

'Fair Philiphaugh, prince, is my ain,

I biggit it wi' lime and stane;

The Tinnies and the Hangingshaw,

My liege, are native steads of mine.

72.

'.   .   .   .   .

.   .   .   .   .

I have mony steads in the forest shaw,

But them by name I dinna knaw.'

73.

The keys of the castle he gave the king,
With the blessing of his fair ladye;
He was made sheriff of Ettrick Forest,
Surely while upward grows the tree;
And if he was not traitour to the king,
Forfaulted he suld never be.

74.

Wha ever heard, in ony times,
Siccan an outlaw in his degree
Sic favour get before a king
As did the Outlaw Murray of the forest free?

SIR ANDREW BARTON

THE TEXT is taken from the Percy Folio MS., but the spelling is modernised. There is another version, extant in broadsides to be found in nearly all the large collections; this, when set beside the Folio MS. text, provides a remarkable instance of the loss a ballad sustained by falling into the hands of the broadside-printers. The present text, despite the unlucky hiatus after st. 35, is a splendid example of an English ballad, which cannot be earlier than the sixteenth century. There is a fine rhythm throughout, and, as Child says, 'not many better passages are met with in ballad poetry than that which tells of the three gallant attempts on the mainmast tree (stt. 52-66).'

THE STORY told in the ballad is a piece of history, and belongs originally to the beginning of the sixteenth century. Andrew Barton was one of three sons of John Barton, a Scots trader whose ship had been plundered by the Portuguese in 1476; letters of reprisal were granted to the brothers Barton, and renewed to them in 1506 'as no opportunity had occurred of effectuating a retaliation.' It seems, however, that this privilege was abused, at least by Andrew, who was reported in June 1511 to Henry VIII. as seizing English ships under the pretext that they were Portuguese. The king did not send Lord Charles Howard, as the ballad states—Lord Charles was not born till twenty-five years afterwards—but Sir Thomas and Sir Edward Howard set out against the pirate by Henry's leave. They took two ships, not one, the meeting with Henry Hunt (st. 18) being the ballad-maker's invention. Lord Charles's fraudulent use of the 'white flag' in st. 37 is supported by Bishop Lesley's partisan account of the engagement, written *c.* 1570. The time-scheme of the ballad is unusually vague: it begins 'in midsummer-time,' and the punitive expedition starts on 'the day before midsummer even'—*i.e.* June 19, which agrees with the chronicles. The fight takes place within the week; but Lord Charles does not get home until December 29 (st. 71). Hall's chronicle says that they returned on August 2.

Lord Charles Howard was created Earl of Nottingham in 1596; but the adoption of this into the ballad (st. 78) dates only our text. It is quite probable that it existed in a previous version with names and facts more correctly stated.

SIR ANDREW BARTON

1.

AS it befell in midsummer-time,

When birds sing sweetly on every tree,
Our noble king, King Henry the Eighth,
Over the river of Thames passed he.

2.

He was no sooner over the river,
Down in a forest to take the air,
But eighty merchants of London city
Came kneeling before King Henry there.

3.

'O ye are welcome, rich merchants,
Good sailors, welcome unto me!'
They swore by the rood they were sailors good,
But rich merchants they could not be.

4.

'To France nor Flanders dare we not pass,
Nor Bordeaux voyage we dare not fare,
And all for a false robber that lies on the seas,
And robs us of our merchant's-ware.'

5.

King Henry was stout, and he turned him about,
And swore by the Lord that was mickle of might;
'I thought he had not been in the world throughout
That durst have wrought England such unright.'

6.

But ever they sighed, and said, alas!
Unto King Henry this answer again;
'He is a proud Scot that will rob us all
If we were twenty ships and he but one.'

7.

The king looked over his left shoulder,

Amongst his lords and barons so free;

'Have I never a lord in all my realm

Will fetch yond traitor unto me?'

8.

'Yes, that dare I!' says my lord Charles Howard,

Near to the king whereas he did stand;

'If that your Grace will give me leave,

Myself will be the only man.'

9.

'Thou shalt have six hundred men,' saith our king,

'And choose them out of my realm so free,

Besides mariners and boys,

To guide the great ship on the sea.'

10.

'I'll go speak with Sir Andrew,' says Charles, my lord Howard,

'Upon the sea, if he be there;

I will bring him and his ship to shore,

Or before my prince I will never come near.'

11.

The first of all my lord did call,

A noble gunner he was one;

This man was three score years and ten,

And Peter Simon was his name.

12.

'Peter,' says he, 'I must sail to the sea,

To seek out an enemy; God be my speed!

Before all others I have chosen thee;
Of a hundred gunners thou'st be my head.'

13.
13.⁴, 16.⁴: 'bread,' breadth.
'My lord,' says he, 'if you have chosen me
Of a hundred gunners to be the head,
Hang me at your main-mast tree
If I miss my mark past three pence bread.'
14.
The next of all my lord he did call,
A noble bowman he was one;
In Yorkshire was this gentleman born,
And William Horsley was his name.
15.
'Horsley,' says he, 'I must sail to the sea,
To seek out an enemy; God be my speed!
Before all others I have chosen thee;
Of a hundred bowmen thou'st be my head.'
16.
'My lord,' says he, 'if you have chosen me
Of a hundred bowmen to be the head,
Hang me at your main-mast tree
If I miss my mark past twelve pence bread.'
17.
With pikes, and guns, and bowmen bold,
This noble Howard is gone to the sea
On the day before mid-summer even,
And out at Thames' mouth sailed they.

18.

They had not sailed days three

Upon their journey they took in hand,

But there they met with a noble ship,

And stoutly made it both stay and stand.

19.

'Thou must tell me thy name,' says Charles, my lord Howard,

'Or who thou art, or from whence thou came,

Yea, and where thy dwelling is,

To whom and where thy ship does belong.'

20.

'My name,' says he, 'is Harry Hunt,

With a pure heart and a penitent mind;

I and my ship they do belong

Unto the New-castle that stands upon Tyne.'

21.

'Now thou must tell me, Harry Hunt,

As thou hast sailed by day and by night,

Hast thou not heard of a stout robber?

Men call him Sir Andrew Barton, knight.'

22.

But ever he sighed and said, 'Alas!

Full well, my lord, I know that wight;

He robbed me of my merchant's-ware,

And I was his prisoner but yesternight.

23.

23.[3] 'arch-board,' stern (?) Cp. 29.[2] and 'hatch-board,' 70.[2].

'As I was sailing upon the sea,

And Bordeaux voyage as I did fare,
He clasped me to his arch-board,
And robbed me of all my merchant's-ware.

24.
'And I am a man both poor and bare,
And every man will have his own of me,
And I am bound towards London to fare,
To complain to my prince Henry.'
25.
'That shall not need,' says my lord Howard;
'If thou canst let me this robber see,
For every penny he hath taken thee fro,
Thou shalt be rewarded a shilling,' quoth he.
26.
'Now God forfend,' says Henry Hunt,
'My lord, you should work so far amiss:
God keep you out of that traitor's hands!
For you wot full little what a man he is.
27.
'He is brass within, and steel without,
And beams he bears in his top-castle strong;
His ship hath ordnance clean round about;
Besides, my lord, he is very well manned.
28.
28.[1] 'dearly dight,' handsomely fitted out.
'He hath a pinnace is dearly dight,
Saint Andrew's cross, that is his guide;
His pinnace bears nine score men and more,

Besides fifteen cannons on every side.

29.

29.² Cp. 23.³ and note.

'If you were twenty ships, and he but one,
Either in arch-board or in hall,
He would overcome you every one,
And if his beams they do down fall.'

30.

'This is cold comfort,' says my lord Howard,
'To welcome a stranger thus to the sea;
I'll bring him and his ship to shore,
Or else into Scotland he shall carry me.'

31.

'Then you must get a noble gunner, my lord,
That can set well with his eye,
And sink his pinnace into the sea,
And soon then overcome will he be.

32.

'And when that you have done this,
If you chance Sir Andrew for to board,
Let no man to his top-castle go;
And I will give you a glass, my lord,

33.

'And then you need to fear no Scot,
Whether you sail by day or by night;
And to-morrow, by seven of the clock,
You shall meet with Sir Andrew Barton, knight.

34.

'I was his prisoner but yesternight,

And he hath taken me sworn,' quoth he;

'I trust my Lord God will me forgive

And if that oath then broken be.

35.

'You must lend me six pieces, my lord,' quoth he,

'Into my ship, to sail the sea,

And to-morrow, by nine of the clock,

Your honour again then will I see.'

36.

And the hatch-board where Sir Andrew lay

Is hatched with gold dearly dight:

'Now by my faith,' says Charles, my lord Howard,

'Then yonder Scot is a worthy wight!

37.

'Take in your ancients and your standards,

Yea, that no man shall them see,

And put me forth a white willow wand.

As merchants use to sail the sea.'

38.

But they stirred neither top nor mast,

But Sir Andrew they passed by.

'What English are yonder,' said Sir Andrew,

'That can so little courtesy?

39.

'I have been admiral over the sea

More than these years three;

There is never an English dog, nor Portingale,

Can pass this way without leave of me.

40.

'But now yonder pedlars they are past,
Which is no little grief to me;
Fetch them back,' says Sir Andrew Barton,
'They shall all hang at my mainmast tree.'

41.

With that the pinnace it shot off,
That my lord Howard might it well ken;
It struck down my lord's foremast,
And killed fourteen of my lord his men.

42.

'Come hither, Simon,' says my lord Howard,
'Look that thy words be true thou said;
I'll hang thee at my mainmast tree
If thou miss thy mark past twelve pence bread.'

43.

Simon was old, but his heart it was bold;
He took down a piece, and laid it full low;
He put in chain yards nine,
Besides other great shot less and moe.

44.

With that he let his gunshot go;
So well he settled it with his eye,
The first sight that Sir Andrew saw,
He saw his pinnace sunk in the sea.

45.

When he saw his pinnace sunk,

Lord! in his heart he was not well.
'Cut my ropes, it is time to be gone;
I'll go fetch yond pedlars back myself!'
46.
When my lord Howard saw Sir Andrew loose,
Lord! in his heart that he was fain.
'Strike on your drums, spread out your ancients;
Sound out your trumpets, sound out amain!'

47.
47.[2] *i.e.* 'wit [ye], howsoever this affair may turn out.'
'Fight on, my men,' says Sir Andrew Barton,
'Weet, howsoever this gear will sway,
It is my lord Admiral of England
Is come to seek me on the sea.'
48.
Simon had a son; with shot of a gun,
Well Sir Andrew might it ken,
He shot it at a privy place,
And killed sixty more of Sir Andrew's men.
49.
Harry Hunt came in at the other side,
And at Sir Andrew he shot then;
He drove down his foremast tree,
And killed eighty more of Sir Andrew's men.
50.
'I have done a good turn,' says Harry Hunt,
'Sir Andrew is not our king's friend;
He hoped to have undone me yesternight,

But I hope I have quit him well in the end.'

51.

'Ever alas!' said Sir Andrew Barton,

'What should a man either think or say?

Yonder false thief is my strongest enemy,

Who was my prisoner but yesterday.

52.

'Come hither to me, thou Gordon good,

And be thou ready at my call,

And I will give thee three hundred pound

If thou wilt let my beams down fall.'

53.

53.[1] 'swarved,' swarmed, climbed

53.[3] 'bearing arrow': perhaps a light arrow for long-distance shooting, but see 56.[3]; and cf. *Adam Bell*, 150.[3].

With that he swarved the mainmast tree,

So did he it with might and main;

Horsley, with a bearing arrow,

Strake the Gordon through the brain.

54.

And he fell into the hatches again,

And sore of this wound that he did bleed;

Then word went through Sir Andrew's men

That the Gordon he was dead.

55.

'Come hither to me, James Hamilton,

Thou art my sister's son, I have no more;

I will give thee six hundred pound

If thou will let my beams down fall.'

56.
With that he swarved the mainmast tree,
So did he it with might and main;
Horsley, with another broad arrow,
Strake the yeoman through the brain.
57.
That he fell down to the hatches again;
Sore of his wound that he did bleed.
Covetousness gets no gain,
It is very true as the Welshman said.

58.
But when he saw his sister's son slain,
Lord! in his heart he was not well.
'Go fetch me down my armour of proof,
For I will to the top-castle myself.
59.
'Go fetch me down my armour of proof,
For it is gilded with gold so clear;
God be with my brother, John of Barton!
Amongst the Portingales he did it wear.'
60.
But when he had his armour of proof,
And on his body he had it on,
Every man that looked at him
Said, gun nor arrow he need fear none.
61.
'Come hither, Horsley,' says my lord Howard,
'And look your shaft that it go right;

Shoot a good shoot in the time of need,
And for thy shooting thou'st be made a knight.'
62.
'I'll do my best,' says Horsley then,
'Your honour shall see before I go;
If I should be hanged at your mainmast,
I have in my ship but arrows two.'
63.
63.³ 'spole,' spauld, shoulder.
But at Sir Andrew he shot then;
He made sure to hit his mark;
Under the spole of his right arm
He smote Sir Andrew quite through the heart.

64.
64.³ 'jack,' coat of mail.
Yet from the tree he would not start,
But he clinged to it with might and main;
Under the collar then of his jack
He strake Sir Andrew through the brain.
65.
'Fight on, my men,' says Sir Andrew Barton,
'I am hurt, but I am not slain;
I'll lay me down and bleed awhile,
And then I'll rise and fight again.
66.
66.⁴ 'Till' may mean 'while.'
'Fight on, my men,' says Sir Andrew Barton,
'These English dogs they bite so low;

Fight on for Scotland and Saint Andrew
Till you hear my whistle blow!'

67.

But when they could not hear his whistle blow,
Says Harry Hunt, 'I'll lay my head
You may board yonder noble ship, my lord,
For I know Sir Andrew he is dead.'

68.

With that they boarded this noble ship,
So did they it with might and main;
They found eighteen score Scots alive,
Besides the rest were maimed and slain.

69.

My lord Howard took a sword in his hand,
And smote off Sir Andrew's head;
The Scots stood by did weep and mourn,
But never a word durst speak or say.

70.

He caused his body to be taken down,
And over the hatch-board cast into the sea,
And about his middle three hundred crowns:
'Wheresoever thou lands, it will bury thee.'

71.

With his head they sailed into England again,
With right good will and force and main,
And the day before New Year's Even
Into Thames' mouth they came again.

72.

My lord Howard wrote to King Henry's grace,
With all the news he could him bring:
'Such a New Year's gift I have brought to your Grace
As never did subject to any king.
73.
'For merchandise and manhood,
The like is not to be found:
The sight of these would do you good,
For you have not the like in your English ground.'
74.
But when he heard tell that they were come,
Full royally he welcomed them home;
Sir Andrew's ship was the king's New Year's gift;
A braver ship you never saw none.

75.
Now hath our king Sir Andrew's ship,
Beset with pearls and precious stones;
Now hath England two ships of war—
Two ships of war, before but one.
76.
'Who holp to this?' says King Henry,
'That I may reward him for his pain.'
'Harry Hunt, and Peter Simon,
William Horsley, and I the same.'
77.
'Harry Hunt shall have his whistle and chain,
And all his jewels, whatsoever they be,
And other rich gifts that I will not name,

For his good service he hath done me.

78.

'Horsley, right thou'st be a knight,

Lands and livings thou shalt have store;

Howard shall be Earl of Nottingham,

And so was never Howard before.

79.

'Now Peter Simon, thou art old;

I will maintain thee and thy son;

Thou shalt have five hundred pound all in gold

For the good service that thou hast done.'

80.

Then King Henry shifted his room.

In came the Queen and ladies bright;

Other errands had they none

But to see Sir Andrew Barton, knight.

81.

But when they see his deadly face,

His eyes were hollow in his head;

'I would give a hundred pound,' says King Henry,

'The man were alive as he is dead!

82.

'Yet for the manful part that he hath played,

Both here and beyond the sea,

His men shall have half a crown a day

To bring them to my brother, King Jamie.'

HENRY MARTYN

THE TEXT is from a copy taken down from North Devon tradition by the Rev. S. Baring Gould, and printed by Child; since when other versions have been found still in circulation in England. A Sussex version, though perhaps derived from a Catnach broadside, is given in the *Journal* of the Folk-Song Society, vol. i. 162.

THE STORY.—This ballad is undoubtedly a degenerate version of the preceding, *Sir Andrew Barton*, of which name, as Child says, Henry Martyn would be no extraordinary corruption. It is given here as an instance of the fate which awaits a popular ballad in the process of being sung to pieces.

HENRY MARTYN

1.

IN merry Scotland, in merry Scotland
There lived brothers three;
They all did cast lots which of them should go
A robbing upon the salt sea.

2.

The lot it fell on Henry Martyn,
The youngest of the three;
That he should go rob on the salt, salt sea
To maintain his brothers and he.

3.

He had not a-sailed a long winter's night,
Nor yet a short winter's day,
Before that he met with a lofty old ship,
Come sailing along that way.

4.

O when she came by Henry Martyn;
'I prithee now, let us go!'

'O no, God wot! that, that will I not,
O that will I never do.

5.

'Stand off, stand off!' said Henry Martyn,
'For you shall not pass by me;
For I am a robber all on the salt seas,
To maintain us brothers three.

6.

'How far, how far,' cries Henry Martyn,
'How far do you make it?' said he;
'For I am a robber all on the salt seas,
To maintain us brothers three.'

7.

For three long hours they merrily fought,
For hours they fought full three;
At last a deep wound got Henry Martyn,
And down by the mast fell he.

8.

'Twas broadside to a broadside then,
And a rain and hail of blows,
But the salt sea ran in, ran in, ran in,
To the bottom then she goes.

9.

Bad news, bad news for old England,
Bad news has come to the town,
For a rich merchant's vessel is cast away,
And all her brave seamen drown.

10.

Bad news, bad news through London Street,

Bad news has come to the king,

For all the brave lives of the mariners lost,

That are sunk in the watery main.

JOHN DORY

THE TEXT is from Ravenscroft's *Deuteromelia* (1609), the only text that has come down to us of a 'three-man's song' which achieved extraordinary popularity during' the seventeenth century.

THE STORY.—'Good King John of France' is presumed to be John II., who was taken prisoner at the battle of Poictiers and died in 1364. But the earliest literary reference to this ballad occurs in the play of *Gammar Gurton's Needle*, acted in 1566, where the song 'I cannot eat but little meat' is to be sung 'to the tune of John Dory.' From Carew's *Survey of Cornwall* (1602) we learn a little more: 'Moreover, the prowess of one Nicholas, son to a widow near Foy [Fowey], is descanted upon in an old three-man's song, namely, how he fought bravely at sea with John Dory (a Genowey, as I conjecture), set forth by John, the French king, and, after much bloodshed on both sides, took, and slew him, in revenge of the great ravine and cruelty which he had fore committed upon the Englishmen's goods and bodies.'

JOHN DORY

1.

AS it fell on a holy-day,

And upon a holy-tide-a,

John Dory bought him an ambling nag

To Paris for to ride-a.

2.

And when John Dory to Paris was come,

A little before the gate-a,

John Dory was fitted, the porter was witted

To let him in thereat-a.

3.

The first man that John Dory did meet

Was good king John of France-a;

John Dory could well of his courtesie,

But fell down in a trance-a.

4.

'A pardon, a pardon, my liege and my king,
For my merry men and for me-a,
And all the churles in merry England,
I'll bring them all bound to thee-a.'

5.

And Nicholl was then a Cornish man
A little beside Bohide-a,
And he manned forth a good black bark
With fifty good oars on a side-a.

6.

'Run up, my boy, unto the main-top,
And look what thou canst spy-a.'
'Who ho, who ho! a goodly ship I do see;
I trow it be John Dory-a.'

7.

They hoist their sails, both top and top,
The mizzen and all was tried-a,
And every man stood to his lot,
What ever should betide-a.

8.

The roaring cannons then were plied,
And dub-a-dub went the drum-a;
The braying trumpets loud they cried
To courage both all and some-a.

9.

The grappling-hooks were brought at length,

The brown bill and the sword-a;

John Dory at length, for all his strength,

Was clapped fast under board-a.

CAPTAIN WARD AND THE RAINBOW

THE TEXT is from a broadside in the Bagford collection (i. 65); other broadsides, very similar, are to be found in the Pepys, Roxburghe, and other collections. The ballad has often been reprinted; and more than one oral version has been recovered—much corrupted in transmission.

THE STORY is apocryphal, as has been shown by research undertaken since Child annotated the ballad; so also are other broadsides, *The Seamen's Song of Captain Ward* and *The Seamen's Song of Dansekar*, which deal with Ward. He was a Kentish fisherman, born at Feversham about 1555, who turned pirate after a short service aboard the *Lion's Whelp* man-of-war. The *Rainbow* was the name of a ship then in the navy, often mentioned in reports from 1587 onwards; but Professor Sir J. K. Laughton has pointed out that she never fought with Ward. Possibly *Rainbow* is a corruption of *Tramontana*, a small cruiser which *may* have chased him once in the Irish Channel. The fullest account of Ward may be found in an article, unsigned, but written by Mr. John Masefield, in the *Gentleman's Magazine* for March, 1906, pp. 113-126.

CAPTAIN WARD AND THE RAINBOW

1.

STRIKE up, you lusty gallants,

With music and sound of drum,

For we have descried a rover

Upon the sea is come;

His name is Captain Ward,

Right well it doth appear,

There has not been such a rover

Found out this thousand year:

2.

For he hath sent unto our King,

The sixth of January,

Desiring that he might come in

With all his company.

'And if your King will let me come

Till I my tale have told,

I will bestow for my ransom,

Full thirty ton of gold.'

3.

'O nay, O nay,' then said our King,

'O nay, this may not be,

To yield to such a rover,

Myself will not agree:

He hath deceived the Frenchman,

Likewise the King of Spain,

And how can he be true to me,

That hath been false to twain?'

4.

With that our King provided

A ship of worthy fame,

Rainbow is she called,

If you would know her name:

Now the gallant Rainbow

She rows upon the sea,

Five hundred gallant seamen

To bear her company.

5.

The Dutchman and the Spaniard,

She made them for to fly,

Also the bonny Frenchman,

As she met him on the sea.

When as this gallant Rainbow

Did come where Ward did lie,
'Where is the captain of this ship?'
This gallant Rainbow did cry.
6.
'O, that am I,' says Captain Ward,
'There's no man bids me lie,
And if thou art the King's fair ship,
Thou art welcome to me.'
'I'll tell thee what,' says Rainbow,
'Our King is in great grief,
That thou shouldst lie upon the sea,
And play the arrant thief,
7.
'And will not let our merchants' ships
Pass as they did before;
Such tidings to our King is come,
Which grieves his heart full sore.'
With that, this gallant Rainbow
She shot, out of her pride,
Full fifty gallant brass pieces
Chargëd on every side.
8.
And yet these gallant shooters
Prevailëd not a pin,
Though they were brass on the outside,
Brave Ward was steel within;

Shoot on, shoot on,' says Captain Ward,
'Your sport well pleaseth me,

And he that first gives over,
Shall yield unto the sea.

9.
'I never wronged an English ship,
But Turk and King of Spain,
For and the jovial Dutchman,
As I met on the main;
If I had known your King
But one-two years before,
I would have saved brave Essex life,
Whose death did grieve me sore.

10.
'Go tell the King of England,
Go tell him thus from me,
If he reigns King of all the land,
I will reign King at sea.'
With that the gallant Rainbow shot,
And shot and shot in vain,
And left the rover's company,
And return'd home again.

11.
'Our royal King of England,
Your ship's returned again,
For Ward's ship is so strong
It never will be ta'en.'
'O everlasting!' says our King,
'I have lost jewels three,
Which would have gone unto the seas
And brought proud Ward to me.

12.

'The first was Lord Clifford,

Earl of Cumberland;

The second was the Lord Mountjoy

As you shall understand;

The third was brave Essex

From field would never flee,

Which would have gone unto the seas,

And brought proud Ward to me.'

THE SWEET TRINITY

THE TEXT is taken from a broadside in the Pepys collection (iv. 196), which can be dated between 1682 and 1685, and is entitled *Sir Walter Raleigh sailing in the Low-lands*. Three other copies of the same edition of the broadside are known.

THE STORY of the *Sweet Trinity* has become confused with that of the *Golden Vanity* (*Golden Victorie*, *Golden Trinitie*, *Gold Pinnatree* are variants), which is probably a corrupted form of it; indeed the weak ending of the broadside challenges any singer to improve upon it. But again there are two distinct variations of the *Golden Vanity* ballad. In the first class, the boy, having sunk the French galley, calls to the *Golden Vanity* to throw him a rope, and when it is refused, threatens to sink her too; whereupon they take him aboard and carry out all their promises of reward (which vary considerably in the different versions). In the second class, the boy dies after he is taken up from the water; in one version he sinks from exhaustion before he can be saved.

The *Sweet Trinity*, however, has been taken by a ship of unspecified nationality ('false' might easily become corrupted into 'French'); and thus this ballad deals with three ships, while the *Golden Vanity* versions mention but two. The latter are still current in folk-song.

THE SWEET TRINITY

1.

SIR WALTER RALEIGH has built a ship,
In the Netherlands;
Sir Walter Raleigh has built a ship,
In the Netherlands;
And it is called the Sweet Trinity,
And was taken by the false gallaly.
Sailing in the Lowlands.

2.

'Is there never a Seaman bold
In the Netherlands;
Is there never a Seaman bold
In the Netherlands;
That will go take this false gallaly,
And to redeem the Sweet Trinity?
Sailing in the Lowlands.

3.

Then spoke the little Ship-boy,
In the Netherlands;
Then spoke the little Ship-boy,
In the Netherlands;
'Master, master, what will you give me,
And I will take this false gallaly,
And release the Sweet Trinity?
Sailing in the Lowlands.

4.

'I'll give thee gold, and I'll give thee fee,

In the Netherlands;

I'll give thee gold, and I'll give thee fee,

In the Netherlands;

And my eldest daughter, thy wife shall be.

Sailing in the Lowlands.'

5.

5.¹ 'set his breast': perhaps this simply means he breasted the water; but see *Glossary of Ballad Commonplaces*, First Series, xlvi.

He set his breast, and away he did swim,

Until he came to the false gallaly.

6.

He had an augur fit for the nonce,

The which will bore fifteen good holes at once.

7.

Some were at cards, and some at dice,

Until the salt water flashed in their eyes.

8.

Some cut their hats, and some cut their caps,

For to stop the salt water gaps.

9.

He set his breast, and away did swim,

Until he came to his own ship again.

10.

'I have done the work I promised to do,

I have sunk the false gallaly,

And released the Sweet Trinity.

11.

'You promised me gold, and you promised me fee,

Your eldest daughter my wife she must be.'

12.

'You shall have gold, and you shall have fee,

But my eldest daughter your wife shall never be.'

13.

'Then fare you well, you cozening Lord,

Seeing you are not so good as your word.'

14.

And thus I shall conclude my song,

Of the sailing in the Lowlands,

Wishing all happiness to all seamen both old and young,

In their sailing in the Lowlands.